D1330017

WITHDRAWAL

The Art of Play

Megan LaMon

Photography by
Megan LaMon

Paintings by
Children of the School District of Philadelphia

The ART OF PLAY

Recess and the Practice of Invention

Anna R. Beresin

Temple University Press Philadelphia

HARVARD UNIVERSITY
GRADUATE SCHOOL OF EDUCATION
MONROE C. GUTMAN LIBRARY

TEMPLE UNIVERSITY PRESS
Philadelphia, Pennsylvania 19122
www.temple.edu/tempress

Copyright © 2014 by Anna R. Beresin
All rights reserved
Published 2014

Library of Congress Cataloging-in-Publication Data

Beresin, Anna R.
  The art of play : recess and the practice of invention / Anna Beresin.
     pages cm
  Includes bibliographical references and index.
  ISBN 978-1-4399-1093-1 (hardback : alk. paper) — ISBN 978-1-4399-1094-8
(paper : alk. paper) — ISBN 978-1-4399-1095-5 (e-book)   1. School recess breaks.
2. Play—United States.   3. Child development.   I. Title.
  LB3033.B48 2013
  371.2'42—dc23

                                                                      2013019862

♾ The paper used in this publication meets the requirements of the American
National Standard for Information Sciences—Permanence of Paper for Printed
Library Materials, ANSI Z39.48–1992

Printed in the United States of America

2 4 6 8 9 7 5 3 1

This one's for **Neilo.**

Contents

The Art of Play

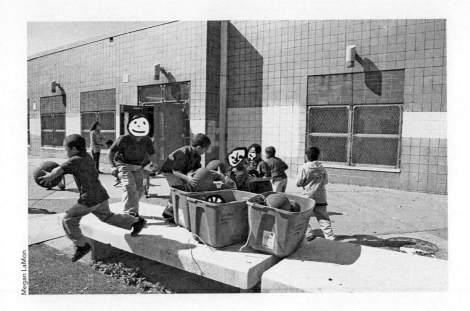
Megan LaMon

Introduction

*I feel sure that we must account for the origin of art by
some reference to play.*
—JAMES SULLY, PSYCHOLOGIST, 1895, 327

*Can I draw on the ground with this chalk?
I'm a really good artist.*
— RAFAEL, AGE 10

From 2010 to 2012 I worked with students from The University of the Arts to donate jump ropes, balls, hoops, and chalk—all traditional urban play materials—to nine public schools in Philadelphia. The idea was to make it possible for resource-poor schools to enrich children's time and to support children's expressive culture. We followed our donation with an art activity in four of the schools, where teachers asked the children to paint what they do at recess and how it makes them feel. Art about play became *The Art of Play*.

Consider the following two paintings (Figures I.1 and I.2). The first, from an earlier study, was painted by an eight-year-old boy enamored with the Harry Potter series (Beresin 2010). When I asked him what he does at recess, he painted "Quidditch," with its snitch, quaffle, and

Figure I.1 (Grade 5)

beater balls. His painting is not an exact copy of a Quidditch pitch: the set on the left copies the proportions of the hoops in the books and movies, but the one on the right has the hoops in their own order, like a diagram of a family or a constellation of friends. It is both an image of Quidditch and not an image of Quidditch. And when I asked him to paint or tell me more, he painted the people he plays with: "Albus Dumbledore, Eva, Tyson, and me."

The second was more recently painted by a ten-year-old girl in a school in West Philadelphia. Because there were no working basketball hoops, the children invented "hoop ball," with hula hoops used as makeshift baskets for shooting basketballs. Earlier that day I had witnessed this exact image on their playground. A group of children gathered around the girl who painted it, nodding their approval of its portrayal and puffing out their chests.

These two paintings and the children who painted them suggest that beyond the social and aerobic benefits of recess, there is a hidden realm of invention being practiced and that observational studies like my own previous work were missing pieces of the puzzle. Some paintings were literal copies of inventions visible on the playground. Some inventions were imaginary and seen only in the children's heads. What can the art of play teach us about the art of play?

The paintings in this book were made by more than one hundred seven-, eight-, nine-, and ten-year-olds. The stories reflect the realities and imaginations of more than two thousand urban lives: Latino children, Asian American children, European American white children, and in the vast majority, African American children. Each chosen school comes from a different part of Philadelphia: North, South, West, Northeast, Northwest, Southeast, East Central, Center City, and Kensington. With one exception, these schools are in working-class neighborhoods, and all the working-class schools have concrete school yards with no built playground equipment of any kind.

The nonprofit Great Schools rates overall school performance on a scale of 1 to 10; these working-class schools earned an average score of 2 out of 10. Several scored 1 out of 10 in terms of poor resources and low test scores.[1] Although some of the schools seemed to belong in a Dickens

Figure I.2 (Grade 5)

novel, many were bright, caring places where a super-heroic staff made do with nonexistent resources. All the schools, administrators, teachers, and children have been given pseudonyms, and all the original art has been returned to the children.

Here are images of leaping, tossing, friendships, and hearts, as well as images of invisible handcuffs. *Broken Song*, a book about the persecution of Russian Jews, waves like a banner to the portrait of Dr. Martin Luther King, Jr. Wished-for breakfast foods join traditional footballs, jump ropes, and basketballs in the flowing ink. The only editing of the paintings was the removal of names, and the collection is shown in its entirety. The paintings are grouped by grade as a developmental cohort, suggesting developmental differences and similarities in children's culture and its portrayal through reflective artistic practice.

Paintlore

Children's cultural historian Brian Sutton-Smith writes of the spontaneous tales that children tell as the "folkstories of children" and their peer

Figure I.3 (Grade 5)

Figure I.4 (Grade 5)

culture outside and in as the "folkgames of children."[2] Folklorist Simon Bronner refers to toys made by children as a form of craft.[3] But chalk and painting present uniquely, becoming what we might term "folk drawings" and "folk paintings." In these images there are themes and styles, frames of reference and frames of perspective. They are created communally in each other's presence.

That first painting of Quidditch led me to view art as a source of documentation of hidden children's culture, and their paintlore as a way to present a host of localized game variations and traditional styles. "Paintlore" is what I call the painted depiction of a culture's folklore done by the people in that particular place. An expressive, communicative art, its main purpose is storytelling.

Folklorist Barbara Kirshenblatt-Gimblett used a collection of paintings to document her father's complex history in prewar Europe, writing: "Like the itinerant patuas of Bengal, who unroll their painted scrolls and perform the stories visualized on them . . . the paintings are not illustrations and the stories are not captions. They are not versions of one another. Rather, different parts of the story are told in different ways in different

Figure I.5 (Grade 5)

media to form a whole that is greater than could be achieved in words or images alone."[4]

Because this book is a folklore study, I focus on the art and the community of creators who make meaning through their art forms. It is not a psychological study of individuals or an institutional study of specific schools. At the center are the emergent play images and play genres, their value as explained by the people in the community and by like-minded thinkers.

In this book we meet Mrs. Dee, the henna-haired gym teacher who dances with the children every day; quiet Ms. Mary, one of the most creative elementary art teachers I have ever met; and school staff who have permanently canceled recess and who believe that "nobody has recess anymore." We hear directly from the children who jumped on these playgrounds along with the recorded observations of games they actually played in front of us. They sang as they played, and sang as they painted, often blurring the activities of art room and playground.

The theme of the practice of invention recurs in the children's own commentary and in the countervoices of practicing adult artists in dance, theater, music, film, design, and fine arts as they think aloud about the play element in their own work. All the children and administrators were participants in Recess Access, a grant-funded initiative of ParLAB, the Philadelphia Applied Research Laboratory at The University of the Arts, where I teach; all the artists quoted are professors of some form of art

Figure I.6 (Grade 5)

Figure I.7 (Grade 5)

Figure I.8 (Grade 5)

there. The book is a pairing of narratives—the telling of the tales of the Recess Access schools from 2010 to 2012 and the examination of the intersection of art and play.

Multiple Meanings

There are many meanings associated with the title *The Art of Play:*

- the art (skill) of being a fine player
- the theoretical connections between art and play itself
- the art images of people at play

Because play is both frame and frame breaker,[5] this book addresses all three meanings and their opposites:

- the art (skill) of being a fine player *and* the creation of skill
- the roots of the arts in play *and* the roots of play in the arts
- the art images of people at play, which will in turn be played with

These abstractions are made concrete, pardon the pun, through the telling of stories emerging from these nine paved urban school yards. The schools were the first in a string of recess advocacy partnerships created with university monies and buoyed by college student labor. Almost all the schools had no playthings of any kind. All donations had no strings attached; school staff members were free to do whatever they wished with the recess and art materials, and each school was eager for more. At the same time, the university students were introduced to neighborhoods in Philadelphia that they had never seen before, most returning for more than one volunteer opportunity. The Recess Access motto: "Give children time. Give children props. Give children a daily recess."

"Props" are "things to play with," like props on a stage that enable storytelling. "Props" are also "support structures" that keep things from falling down. In urban slang, "props" means "proper respect." When given to children, props can validate their practices, uphold their budding friendships, and invite artistic thinking.

Figure I.9 (Grade 5)

Figure I.10 (Grade 5)

Figure I.11 (Grade 5)

Figure I.12 (Grade 5)

The Intersection of Art and Play

Art and play have both been utilized therapeutically with children, and there is an enormous literature to support their use but little on their intersection. A growing literature about skill at play, or "master players," describes resiliency in children,[6] as well as the play connection to creativity in master artists.[7] Typically, these are studies of very young children or of expert artists looking back on their careers.

In his masterwork, *The Ambiguity of Play*, Brian Sutton-Smith writes of the romantic linking of play and art at the turn of the twentieth century:

> When we consider that children's art and modern art were constantly paralleled at the turn of this century, the strength of the linkage between the child's imagination and the child as artist becomes apparent. . . . Leading modern artists, such as Picasso, [Henri] Matisse, [Juan] Gris, [Wassily] Kandinsky, and [Paul] Klee, avowed that they would like to be able to draw like children, because children draw what they imagine and not what they see. . . .
>
> In psychology, since [Karl] Groos at the turn of the century, occasional attempts have been made to separate play and art. . . . For Groos, play is biology and art is culture. For [Daniel] Berlyne . . . play is frivolous and art is revered. . . . [Howard] Gardner sees play in terms of the mastery of anxiety, self, and the world, but art in terms of the mastery of symbolic forms.[8]

Yet Howard Gardner notes:

> Despite the many intervening years, the analogies between the art of the child and the art of the master seem worth cherishing. For it is in the activity of the young child—his preconscious sense of form, his willingness to explore and to solve problems that arise, his capacity to take risks, his affective needs which must be worked out in a symbolic realm—that we find the crucial seeds of the greatest artistic achievement.[9]

Play becomes art in song, drama, dance, sculpture, and drawing. Hear it in the playground's jump-rope rhymes, in the pretend play, the sporting

touch Down

Figure I.13 (Grade 5)

Figure I.14 (Grade 5)

elegance, and the children's attempts to modify their own play environments. Unlike psychologist Howard Gardner and art historian Jonathan Fineberg and the vast majority of writers who address art and childhood,[10] this book focuses on the art of childhood proper, not early childhood or children's artistic genius.

Writers in the field of play studies and in the field of art history have cautioned against the conflation of art and play.[11] Play is not the same as art, as art implies an exacting mastery, yet there are masterful moments in play, and playful moments in the process of creation. What do play and art have in common?

Children's artistry, like all art that comes from a different culture, is often misunderstood, undervalued, and even oppressed. Art history professor Nancy Heller tells me: "What's always bothered me in art history—things that are funny get no respect. Play and humor—at least in the world of art history, there's this belief that anything that was humorous was not worthwhile. . . . It took a while for artists such as [Alexander] Calder to be taken seriously. It's because he is funny, child-like. It took a long time for art historians to accept him as an artist with a capital 'A.' To me, play has the implication of pleasure; by definition it is something you don't have to do; it's therefore suspect."[12]

In 1895 James Sully suggested:

> They build their sand castles, they pretend to keep shop, to enter-tain visitors, and so forth, for the sake of the enjoyment that they find in these actions. This clearly involves one point of kinship with the artist, for the poet sings and the painter paints because they love to do so.
>
> It is evident, moreover, from what was said about the imagina-tive side of play that it has this further circumstance in common with art-production, that it is the bodying forth of a mental image into the semblance of outer life.[13]

This "bodying forth of a mental image" that emerges in play can be found in the children's paintings and in the photos—in the extended chest, the elastic arms, the exaggerated muscles, the leaping forms. If, as philosopher Mark Johnson suggests,[14] the origin of imaginative thinking is in the movements of the body, then the body's movement, with all its cultural stylizations, must be at the root of both play and artistic think-ing. Sigmund Freud, too, was intrigued by the connections between art and play: "Might we not say that every child at play behaves like a creative writer, in that he creates a world of his own, or rather, rearranges the things of his world in a new way which pleases him?"[15]

But unlike the neo-Freudians, who saw play as a form of emotional mastery, I am suggesting that there are a host of practices that are being reinvented during play: the practice of fine and large motor skills; the practice of balance; the practice of friendship; the practice of culture, and with it the practice of words, of singing, drawing, dancing, acting; the practice of design, of expansion and contraction; the practice of juxtaposi-tion; the practice of practice.

Gardner clarifies: "Both young children and adult artists are willing, even eager, to explore their medium, to try out various alternatives, to permit unconscious processes of play to gain sway. . . . Moreover, both are willing to suspend (for somewhat different reasons) their knowledge of what others do, to go their own way, to transcend the practices and boundaries that overwhelm and inhibit 'literal-age' children (and, quite possibly, lesser artists)."[16]

Figure I.15 (Grade 5)

Figure I.16 (Grade 5)

Figure I.17 (Grade 5)

Figure I.18 (Grade 5)

Yet art does not disappear in middle childhood; we just have been looking for children's art in the wrong places. Although it abounds in early childhood, and for some lucky few lasts through adulthood, it has been there all this time—on the playground.

Collecting children's playground art on a large scale has always been the goal of the folklorists of childhood. Collections typically focus on songs, jokes, and rules of games, with collectors recording variations with pen and paper and, later on, with audio and video. Like Sutton-Smith in New Zealand, Iona and Peter Opie surveyed the whole of Great Britain's evolving children's traditions, adding an emphasis on material culture— the toys and things that were designed by and for children. Before them there was Lady Alice B. Gomme (1894), whose methods were limited to what could be collected through letter writing, while in the United States, William Wells Newell gathered games and songs of American children through observation in the 1880s. All these early survey collections were utilized as demonstrations of nationalism and the attempt to discern cultural boundary making through play.

Other scholars of play have been interested in movement across boundaries. Onwuchekwa Jemie collected African American children's

Figure I.19 (Grade 5)

Figure I.20 (Grade 5)

lore in the 1960s and 1970s and found the roots of American verbal play in African verbal arts by comparing recorded words and phrases across the ocean.[17] All collections of children's folklore, from June Factor's "kid-speak" to Kathryn Marsh's collections of singing games in Australia, have in common a sense of the *changing yet consistent* vital play of childhood, seeking the rhymes of the times.[18] Folklorists tend to see children's play as a unique subculture, even as it parodies the adults around them. Yet in order to understand the psychology of creativity within children's culture, we need to examine the larger frames of power.

The Play of the Book

Part I, "Erasing Children's Expressivity," describes the removal of children's opportunities for play and art and the attempts to initiate their return. The focus is on the children's fleeting accessibility to play materials and the children's commentaries as they look at their own paintings. These interactions were recorded before the widespread cuts to Philadelphia art programs in 2013, and if current predictions are validated, children will continue to face not only decreased exposure to any art opportunity in school but also widespread further elimination of recess. Part II, "Master Players," is framed by basic props—chalk, ball, and rope—while introducing the more joyous Recess Access stories. The voices of master artists currently at play in visual art, theater, music, and dance serve as interludes. The artists speak of play in their own practice of improvisation and composition, and of their early memories of playing with art. The contrast suggests that similar processes are at play in the studio and in the playground, that seemingly trivial moves are a part of creative practice.

Part III, "Balancing Acts," shifts from qualitative to quantitative study, analyzing movement with pedometers and paintings by theme. The most academic section of the book, Part III offers wisdom from well-known artists and scholars, from choreographer Rudolf Laban to philosopher John Dewey, from folklorist Henry Glassie to psychologist Robert Coles. The book then appeals for the protection of something I call "children's cultural vitality" and returns to the intersection of art and play.

As we watched the exuberant use of our donations in both the playground and the art room, photography major Megan LaMon asked the school staff if it would be possible to take photographs and then solicit permission for each one. After a year of attempting to secure parental permission for the photographs, we ultimately were unable to publish the images unretouched. Securing widespread parental permission in busy working-class lives is difficult, particularly in American schools. So we solved our dilemma by literally masking the children's identities with faces from the paintings made by the children themselves and then getting staff approval. In this way the raw emotion and expressive physicality is shared without identities being compromised.

As seems fitting in a book called *The Art of Play,* the children's faces are *the children's faces,* masked and real, a surreal documentation of children's culture. In a truly collaborative effort, Recess Access volunteers prepared hundreds of materials, hauled them to schools, scrubbed inky brushes, cleaned desks, and surveyed neighborhood school yards. The children painted what they wished, and then Megan LaMon attached their handpainted faces to their photographed bodies. Not all images are pleasant, just as not all play is sweet, but difficult stories can be enacted in honorable ways. These seven-, eight-, nine-, and ten-year-olds have outlined their play for us in black and white.

Figure I.21 (Grade 5)

Megan LaMon

Erasing Children's Expressivity

CHAPTER 1

"We Don't Have It"

School #1

"We don't *have* recess," the administrator said on the phone. "Not after lunch?" "Not at all." I wait, and count the seconds to see how she responds further. "We do have gym. Some get it once a week, some more than once." We agreed that we could deliver the donated materials to the gym teacher. As we place Recess Access brochures in the toy buckets, we talk of how it could tickle some kind of interest.

Our van circles the school block in the southwest section of the city, a depressed area with overlapping Asian immigrant communities within a larger Italian American community. There is indeed a fenced school yard, a decent size, but it is filled with teachers' parked cars. I was told that the teachers use it to keep their cars safe. Across the street, a butcher shop is filled with caged squawking chickens. Squeaks from the children emerge through the school's basement windows, also covered in wire. Children and chickens in pens.

We are welcomed, and yet sternly reminded, "We don't have recess here." Staff members say it at least three times but appreciatively accept the materials on behalf of the gym teacher. I ask about the parking

Figure 1.1 (Grade 5)

lot. The administrator explains that the surface is rough concrete and that, in order to "protect the children," the staff had removed recess completely. The surface looks only slightly cracked to our eyes. On the way out I notice a lovely protected courtyard in the center of the school building, quite small but smoothly paved. I compliment them on their courtyard and ask if it could be used for recess. "It is used by the pre-schoolers only." "It is too small for big kids." I wonder aloud if small groups could be allowed to use it. "We don't have that kind of staff," say the three aides lingering in the hallway. "Anyway, most schools don't have recess anymore." I counter that this idea is not quite true but wish them well. The administrator takes my card, and the students and I exit. On the way out is a lovely adult-painted mural. It shows young children in a variety of costumes—a serious-looking ballerina, a clown, a scientist, and ironically, a single child holding a playground ball, whistle around his neck.

Administrators in several schools have told us that they cancel recess for punishment or for "enrichment." Never before have I heard that the canceling of children's time to play was for the children's own safety.

There is a common idea that play is necessary for early childhood, for children under five, and that children as "old" as ten "do not need to play." For many adults, recess means "chaos" and children getting hurt.

School #2

The ten-year-olds in our next school in West Philadelphia circle the yard menacingly. They have nothing, almost nothing, to play with, one or two balls brought from home and a lone hula hoop. Hundreds of children push and shove, bang into each other, using each other's bodies for stimulation. The store across the street advertises its WIC food stamp acceptance, and the school yard, hot and gray, has a fenced-in cooling system that parodies a climbing structure in its center.

We are greeted with expectation by a highly efficient administrator who speaks the lingo of schools of education. She says how needed the materials are and tells us that she is in the process of starting a "socialized recess" program at her school. I ask what she means by socialized recess, and she explains that she will be having her fifth-graders lead games for the K–2 recess, which she says is really out of control. Children are vio-

Figure 1.2 (Grade 5)

Figure 1.3 (Grade 5)

lent, getting hurt. She experimented with it and found fewer incidents requiring the nurse's attention. She goes on to explain that her version of socialized recess allows for child choice. If children change their mind, they can change games. "Socialized recess" used to mean color-coded wristbands indicating which games were sanctioned in restricted, designated areas. She said she hopes she does not have to resort to that. She is, however, considering it for next year.

Figure 1.4 (Grade 5)

Figure 1.5 (Grade 5)

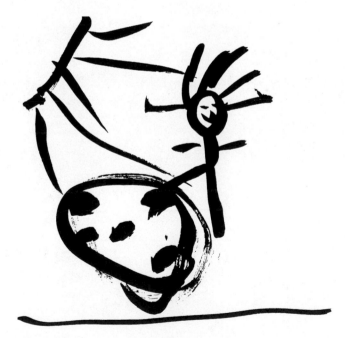

Figure 1.6 (Grade 5)

Figure 1.7 (Grade 5)

She allows us to view the first recess, for the littlest ones, and she holds onto the balls and ropes, not distributing them yet. We watch as the children pull and bang onto each other. One little girl has brought a tangled rope from home. She and her friends sing, "Ice cream, ice cream, in a dish, / How many pieces do you wish?" and I imagine what ice cream looks like in pieces. Several boys climb the pointy fence that guards the ventilation cooling system, even as it emits even more hot air and squealing noise. Its only feature, besides the spikes around it, is a "Danger Keep Off" sign. They have no balls, no toys, and only the one rope, brought from home. The children mostly ram into each other; some get hurt.

Figure 1.8 (Grade 5)

When we return several months later, staff members are pulling a ladder out to reattach the basketball hoop we donated. They set it up each day so it does not get stolen.

Dozens of children exuberantly chase the moving footballs and kickballs we brought last school year. An aide turns one end of the rope as the children sing, "Ice cream, ice cream, cherry on top." The song has shifted, and the school yard has radically changed. Last school year there were no materials and the only activity was climbing the fenced-in heating unit

Figure 1.9 (Grade 5)

Figure 1.10 (Grade 5)

Figure 1.11 (Grade 5)

Figure 1.12 (Grade 5)

that sits in the middle of the school yard. Eighteen children are now occupied by one moving, blue, foam football, tossing it between two loosely organized waving teams.

Revisiting the schools became an opportunity to see how they were doing with our donations and to offer children the chance to paint their recess activities as a form of documentation. After painting his picture of football, one boy takes several small brushes and bounces them like an airy ball to see the effect of his brush marks on the paper, like energetic snow (Figure 1.13). One girl shows me her painting of chase: "We play cops 'n' robbers. See the handcuffs? They're pretend" (Figure 1.14).

A group of girls surround another who is painting elegant jump-rope lines, and I ask them what they sing (Figure 1.15). "We sing 'Nike.'" I ask, is it "Nike, Nike, who can do the Nike?" and they join in, giggling: "FOOT to the N-I-K-E. And HOP to the N-I-K-E." "We sing 'Girl Scout, Girl Scout, Do Your Duty,' 'Challenge, Challenge,' both fast and slow versions, and 'Double Dutch to the World, Foot Hop, Criss, and Walk.'" "We play *everything*," one fifth-grader gushes.

Figure 1.13 (Grade 5)

Figure 1.14 (Grade 5)

Figure 1.15 (Grade 5)

Yet another year later, I sit in the car for a few minutes, watching the same West Philadelphia playground as I return for another art-as-storytelling activity. I see only two footballs, both brought from home. One rope. There is nothing visible from our donation last year. Kids are grabbing each other, roughly tagging. One boy opens the large gate to retrieve a girl's shoe, a slipper much like Cinderella's. When he tries to reenter, his classmates have literally locked him out. They wait. He waits.

After wiggling the gate, he manages to let himself in. The motif "getting locked out" is repeated in two other places along the fence.

One of the gate-keeping boys stares at me. His friend waves. I wave. I unpack the soon-to-be-donated art supplies and walk over to greet them. "Hi," they say. I ask if they ever have any balls to play with—footballs, basketballs, and things like that. "People kept stealing them, and they don't let us have them no more."

Two aides walk over and greet me and notice my UARTS hoodie, and they smile when I say I'm going to meet with Ms. B., the art teacher. I ask the girls what they sing now, and they chorus: "Ice cream, ice cream, in a dish, / How many boyfriends do you wish?"

The aides start singing a new one, and the children and I join in:

LOOK at that GIRL in the MINISKIRT,
You MESS with HER, get your FEELINGS hurt.
She KNOWS karate from the FRONT to the BACK,
WHOOP, she THINKS she's ALL that.

Figure 1.16 (Grade 5)

Figure 1.17 (Grade 5)

Figure 1.18 (Grade 5)

We share a laugh. I ask about materials. They shake their heads. "The only rope there," the aide says, "is the one I brought." As the children all noisily, hysterically, and restlessly return to the building, a teacher's tortured high-pitched shriek echoes in the hallway. "You are not allowed to scream!" she screams.

The optimistic young art teacher of a year ago has wilted. She portions out thimblefuls of paint for an activity that many find limited and boring. One quiet, heavy-set child, Darnell, is sitting motionless while others draw. "I don't like to draw," he mumbles as he stares at a small scissors nearby. After checking with the teacher, I suggest that during our activity he can cut the paper if he wishes. He comes to life with a flurry of cutting, cutting, cutting and produces a tiger face, a sports car, and a "Lemo" (limo), which he labels. I tell him about Matisse, the famous artist whose paper cuts hang in museums. Darnell's eyes widen and he cuts and cuts, furiously and also delicately.

The children write comments on their paintings of what they do at recess:

"My skills I have: play fight, eat food, jump rope"
One smiling stick figure with hearts says, "I want 2 fight"
"Best NFL player"
"Philly 215"
"Nice throw"
"I'm gonna catch it! I hope he catches it"
"The thing I like to do is playing tennis"
"Where's the dogs? Where am I? Your with wild dogs!"
"Nice catch"
"I be your friend"
"I'm having fun!!" (jumping rope)
Heart
NBA names: "D Rose #1, Kobe, #2 L. James, #6K Irving #2R.
    Ron K Garnet #5."
"I will be with . . . Ben . . and Mike. . . . I'll play against Desmon"
    (and in his thought bubble are professionals with helmets and
    a coach)
"DJ Proud"
"Shout out to label"
"I love you"
"I got the ball" "And they say, Get her!"
"Go"
"Help children plz. Let your Voice go Out"

I unroll a mural of their own paintings from the year before and invite them to add captions to these images. This is my way to open the painting up for conversation, to see and hear what they are thinking about as they reflect on their reflections. Over an image of football, one boy writes: "I hope he catches the ball. He probably thinks I can catch. I've never caught a ball in my life." Over a jump-rope line appear the comments "Let's see

who can do more" and "She can jump! Girlscout, Nike, Do Ya, Do Ya."
The abstract image of brush strokes leads to "Fame: My Fans Are My
Everything."

They recognize the image one boy painted of Martin Luther King, Jr. A
small and thoughtful fifth-grader had painted King when he thought about
what he plays on his playground (Figure 1.19). I think of the boy across
town, seven years earlier, who painted his playmate, Albus Dumbledore.
Above Martin Luther King's image, these students painted, "Martin Luther
King Rocks," "Black People," and "I had a Dream." Past tense.

Figure 1.19 (Grade 5)

CHAPTER 2

"Kids Don't Know
How to Play"

School #3

The vice principal in a Northwest Philadelphia school was cautious over the phone. "Kids don't know how to play." He said that they would be happy to accept the materials but that the staff would need to sort through them first. The children would not be playing with them right away. Although serious-sounding by phone, in person he looked about age seven when he peered into the buckets. "It's like Christmas in June!" He told me that most of their playground materials had been stolen three years ago and were never replaced. Now the children have only ropes and a few balls, and only on Fridays. Although the school is housed in an industrial-looking building in a bleak commercial area, there is a bright mural of Barack and Michelle Obama with the word "Hope" right outside the office. The yard is flat, empty—with one painted hopscotch, a tiny foursquare, and a mural of the school's football team name. Like most of the other schools in our program, this K–8 serves five hundred children.

Three times, he and his colleague state, "These children don't know how to play." The staff members like their Friday "socialized recess." When I ask what that means, they tell me that there are zones for each

Figure 2.1 (Grade 4)

Figure 2.2 (Grade 4)

Figure 2.3 (Grade 4)

Figure 2.4 (Grade 4)

game, but they don't enforce the old idea of sticking to one zone or wearing a ribbon or bracelet indicating the pre-chosen activity. We chat about how busy children appear to play well.

Two years later, there are three footballs in play, three basketballs. The donated hoop is up. Three double-dutch ropes and a single rope are in motion. Tennis balls bounce off walls for wall ball; they had none of these before. The children run out of the building and jump quickly and with intensity. One boy does continuous backflips just for the sheer joy of it. There is screaming here—it is of exuberance, and the staff appears

Figure 2.5 (Grade 4)

Figure 2.6 (Grade 4)

relaxed. It has the feel of a beach day, with none of the anger and frustration of the previous school, which lacked the stimulation of play props, although the schools have the same demographics, the same union, and the same curriculum.

School #4

A fourth school, in North Philadelphia, went through several stages: first it had nothing, then its students played with the materials we donated, then

Figure 2.7 (Grade 4)

Figure 2.8 (Grade 4)

Figure 2.9 (Grade 4)

its recess was removed, and then play was restored once again. Like many other schools, it had a cycle of recess removal as punishment, with whole grades of children missing their recess on any given day. Before our art activity, we arrived to witness a hundred or so children marched outside, head behind head, to stand glumly without playing, for twenty minutes. Today there was no recess, this time due to trouble in the overcrowded lunchroom. The children do not know how long they will be punished.

As the children fidget head behind head, I ask a school-yard aide if they use the donated materials for recess. She replies sadly, "What materials?" Surprised that there were any donations six months before, she suggests that I go ask the gym teacher. When I ask the gym teacher if she knows about the donation, she admits that she is saving the materials for gym; she says that she knows they were designated for recess but she lets only a few out at a time. She is afraid the materials will disappear. After an entire recess was spent with more than a hundred children standing still in line, the children are soberly marched to their classrooms while a teacher admires their self-control. One energetic girl takes two steps at a time up the stairs and is yelled at to walk properly.

Figure 2.10 (Grade 4)

Figure 2.11 (Grade 4)

Figure 2.12 (Grade 4)

At our most recent visit to this same school, recess has just started in the main yard and there are about eighty fourth- or fifth-grade boys outside. The main activity for ten minutes is a rough version of tag and play fighting, with several ambiguous episodes involving angry-looking victims. Children are in headlocks; others are thrown to the ground. Almost every time, someone offers a hand back up, usually with an urgent plea to just get up off the ground. There is only one overworked aide outside, and she seems to be in charge of yelling. The main activity appears to be pushing and dodging being pushed. When one really hostile pair begin to escalate their rough-and-tumble gestures, the aide hollers to them, "Think about what you are doing!"

A class of older boys and girls walk through the yard to the side yard with their teacher. They carry two of our newer orange basketballs, a football, and several double-dutch jump ropes, and immediately get busy, leading to a mixed-gender game of half-court, a boys-only version of half-court, and a competitive yet instructional rope session. Several girls lean on the fence and observe the others. A dozen of the younger boys come over to flirt and chat through the fence.

Figure 2.13 (Grade 4)

Figure 2.14 (Grade 4)

Figure 2.15 (Grade 4)

Figure 2.16 (Grade 4)

Figure 2.17 (Grade 4)

Figure 2.18 (Grade 4)

Figure 2.19 (Grade 4)

Figure 2.20 (Grade 4)

All of a sudden, a younger boys' football game begins with twenty players, then thirty, then thirty-five. As props arrive, the pushing dissipates. About twenty continue to dodge and weave and play tag, and another twenty or so linger and chat. Two younger boys play with the wall of the school building, investigating its crevices. Balls are tossed and caught, tossed and caught. Ropes are jumped over and turned, over and turned. A clear correlation seems to emerge: self-organized play with traditional toys decreases rough play, and spurs more and more self-organization by the children. Once the materials are there, the children respond to the props' open invitation. They know what to do and get busy practicing.

PART II

Megan LaMon

Master Players

Megan LaMon

Interlude A

A conversation with visual artists Phillip Schulman and Carol Moore, a husband-and-wife team. Both are known for their playful approach to art materials—from paint to film to design.

Phillip Schulman:

Chalk. Chalk was my favorite thing in the world when I was seven. . . . From the time I was ten years old, I knew what I wanted to be. I did art without thinking of it as play, just as fun. There was the color of it, the typography, the music of it—I was excited by it.

As a child, play is the most wonderful freeing experience, like drawing with crayons, with no other intention than to enjoy yourself. Your intention—a tree, mother, cat—you stay in that space until you lose the willingness to stay. It's almost like the brush, or clay, is moving you. That's a playful scary feeling. On the one hand, this is very fun. Am I really responsible for this? Or is it some outside force? If so, can I do it again?

Carol Moore:

You can't begin to have an artistic process unless it begins with play. You can have an idea, something you want to do—and then think, and play with the materials, with the approach, with strategy—physically moving things around. I'm always moving things around, like these small studies; out of that comes more serious work.

I was eleven or twelve; all I knew was I wanted to be an artist. My mother and father got me a paint-by-number kit for Christmas. I'll never forget it was Old Gloucester, a boat yard, water. I wanted to do it my way, and mix my own paints. This isn't water! How can I make it look like water? My mother didn't approve, she wanted me to follow instructions. I remember the moment—that moment, mixing and layering was so much fun. . . . What were the boundaries? When you are feeling creative, you push.

They discuss whether there is always a story, a narrative, driving art or play.

Carol Moore:

As a grownup, I think it changes, the urges are different, there may not be any narrative. I may keep a piece for years; perhaps it completes an internal narrative. The narrative may be about the composition. I'm playing with the relationship in color or line.

Phillip Schulman:

The goal is to fill the space, the feet of film, to look for a happy accident.

Carol adds:

Other things are always coming into play. Art making is not a linear thing. On the way, the trip, the discovery that occurs, that's the key. It's very much like life. You locate and dislocate yourself at the same time. There's nothing there; then somehow by getting yourself lost, you find yourself.

CHAPTER 3

Chalk

OMG (Hopskach) LOL
—GIRLS READING THEIR CHALK HOPSCOTCH

Chalk was once a staple, a regular tool of urban playgrounds for generations. Philadelphia public schools have eliminated the use of chalk, as it is perceived to be connected to graffiti, even though chalk is an impermanent, washable tool. Hopscotch, foursquare, tic-tac-toe, doodling, and spontaneously written poetry—these have all but disappeared on the playground with the loss of chalk. In some urban playgrounds, school officials have painted a few hopscotches for the children to use, but children need to move their games, expand them, or change them as they see fit, and the painted official forms are often left unused. Some programs import adult play coaches and have the adults draw games with chalk. Our goal was to put chalk back into the hands of children.

School #5

Although it is flanked by two homeless shelters, the Field School in North Philadelphia is a cheery, bright, and earnest place. We are greeted warmly by Mr. Woodson, who seems to be in charge of everything outside classroom instruction, and he holds on to the new basketball hoop with the excitement of a ten-year-old. He has plans to renovate the rooftop yard of this K–8 school, and this seems to be just what he's been wanting. He

Figure 3.1 (Grade 4)

explains that this school does not seem to have the troubles that other schools do in the neighborhood because so many of the children here have parents who also attended the Field School. Many of the same teachers are still here, he says, "so if someone has to call a parent, they are known."

He proudly shows us the concrete slab that is their main school yard. It is clean, evenly smooth, with a few hopscotches painted on. There are a few hoops, but many are missing, and the lanky poles look like awkward teenagers. He grins as he opens each tub of donated goods. "Oh, the boys will love those footballs." "Dodgeballs," he chuckles. "Ropes, ooh. Chalk? The little ones, I'll save that for the littles."

We bounce down the stairs to the yard and watch the K–2s emerge. They stand in clumps and clearly have no materials to play with. A few hold hands and run. A small cluster of girls clap a numbers game. They stand and shift from one leg to another. Then, like opening a faucet, Mr. Woodson tosses the yellow and blue playground balls to clumps of children. He lobs a football and a basketball to the boys in a sectioned-off area. He places chalk gingerly on the ground. Ropes come out, and the place comes alive.

Figure 3.2 (Grade 4)

Figure 3.3 (Grade 4)

Chalk, the forbidden substance, leads to tic-tac-toe. He notices that they do not know how to draw one properly and fixes their board by adding another row of boxes. Little girls draw figures and sign their names. One writes, "Boys are glwy" and gets her chalk taken away, but the rest keep drawing. Some draw houses. Like water on the hot concrete, the toys refresh the children. Mr. Woodson says, "We've got to let kids be kids." A dedicated worker, he confides that he has a seven-year-old and a five-year-old who will be going to school for the first time this fall. He wants to treat children the way he wishes his own children to be treated.

The children mark the ground with color, dashing and stroking the concrete, giggling at the pleasure of mark making, and the surprise of marks that shape into meaning. Dashes lead to lines, lines lead to shapes, and then narratives emerge: homes in a place of homelessness, friendships, hearts, the practice of names and games. As sociologist Roger Caillois wrote, "What is expressed in play is no different from what is expressed in culture."[1] For historian Johan Huizinga, "All poetry is born of play."[2]

Figure 3.4 (Grade 4)

Figure 3.5 (Grade 4)

The girls who drew the hopscotches drew them side by side, with "OMG" and "LOL," and did not play on them but presented them as art. The six-year-olds who drew images of homes in a school flanked by homeless shelters practiced emotional and social sophistication. The numerous chalked love letters to favorite teachers and best friends, names in cursive with hearts drawn—these are performed displays with no need for advanced technique. Chalk is temporary, like childhood itself: fleeting, but rich with happy accidents, juxtapositions like a smiling fish on concrete.

Just as there are master artists, there are, among children, master players. A fine athlete can be a "ball hog" and not take turns or pass the ball. A fine artist can break all the chalk. But a master player manages the play moment in conjunction with everyone else to keep the play alive. Master players often use humor, gentle touch, distraction, and reason to avoid conflict, as long as the game is exciting and stimulating enough. Sometimes conflicts can be settled by children with master-player status more quickly than by grown-ups, however caring the grown-ups may be.[3]

Figure 3.6 (Grade 4)

Figure 3.7 (Grade 4)

Figure 3.8 (Grade 4)

Tanya trades chalk colors with her friends and sees that the trading is fair. Jimmy and Rakim have master status on the basketball court. Theirs is a combined list of athletic skill, grace, and perceived fairness. The master rope jumpers are often the keepers of the singing tradition. They know the most songs and mix the humility of guidance for the younger ones with the bravado of singing loudly and doing complicated turns. Kia tells the littler girl to try the rope again and keeps the intruders at bay. Vicky indicates to Maya to turn the rope more slowly for the awkward jumper. Mr. Goodson nonverbally uses his relationship with the master players to keep the games going, knowing that these children have the respect of their peers and by extension will respect him.

When we return to the Field School, armed with reams of paper, brushes, and India ink, the children are patient and eagerly await their art materials. After some encouragement the ink waters open, and they, like the children of the other schools, are unstoppable. They paint portraits, with bulging muscles, a Muslim headscarf, tiny portraits and large bold ones, one with hearts and stars and one self-labeled "ugly." After his portrait, one writes, "SOS." As they paint a jump rope, they sing for me while they paint:

ICE cream, ICE cream, CHERRY on TOP,
HOW many BOYfriends DO you GOT?

Challenge, challenge,
Girl Scout, Girl Scout, do your duty.

One girl notes that as they paint, her neighbor is "expressing her feelings." Another sings for me:

JOHNNY over the OCEAN,
JOHNNY over the SEA,
JOHNNY stole the MILK cart and BLAMED it on ME.
I told MAMA, MAMA told PAPA,
JOHNNY got BEAT with the RED hot PEPPER.

Some paint their pages black; others, when no one is looking, dip their fingers in the cool India ink, making dots and dashes and doodles on their paper and on their skin.[4]

Philadelphia public schools do not have access to paper—paper for drawing, for practicing math problems, for writing practice, paper for thinking. At each of our visits, the children work with each donated sheet as if it is a delicacy, and their ideas pour out like black icing. As in the chalk drawings of the school yard, the major themes are identity, friendship, and exuberant movement.

Figure 3.9 (Grade 4)

Figure 3.10 (Grade 4)

Just as play pushes boundaries, so master players are occasional troublemakers.[5] In every art class, there are children who sneakily paint their hands and add handlebar mustaches to their faces. They are gently warned that India ink is difficult to wash off, that it will stain their clothing if they are not careful. Girls and boys dip fingers and whole hands furtively in the dark pools and are sent out to wash. One girl jokes about her paper being "under there." "Under where?" is the response, and the girl slaps her knees, giggling at the forbidden word. "She said 'underwear,' hee hee hee."

At the end of the painting session, we transfer the leftover ink into a small bucket to repour into the original container, careful not to waste a drop, as instructed by the teacher. The room and children are ready for their next class, and one fifth-grader, Tanya, quickly dips her washed hands into the last pool of un-recycled ink, giving me a sly look and a silent "please don't tell." I quietly hand her a paper to blot her hands so the ink will not touch her clothes, and with her head taller than when she entered, she takes the blackness with her.

Figure 3.11 (Grade 4)

Figure 3.12 (Grade 4)

Figure 3.13 (Grade 4)

Chalk and Mirror

This week's team of student volunteers included a budding filmmaker, a painter, and several industrial designers. Because we were in the neighborhood, we stopped by the Village of the Arts and Humanities for inspiration.[6] The Village began as a mural project and sculpture garden in a neighborhood filled with despair and with one of the highest unemployment rates in the city. A wall across from the first garden is graffiti-tagged "Little Beirut," yet despite the neighborhood's violent reputation, we are greeted warmly. We looked at the boldly colored mosaics, created and inspired by master painter Lily Yeh, and talked about art and accidental activism. While Professor Yeh was clearing out a trash-filled yard for sculpture, she was offered a hand by some unemployed men and soon joined by the children in the neighborhood, curious about all the activity. A movement grew, and the Village of the Arts and Humanities is now a multiblock site of gardens with vibrant mosaics, offering after-school arts classes and public health programs.

The Village takes broken pieces and then works with artists to put itself back together. Rivers of tile grace garden paths, benches, and homes; artificial mosaic trees join memorials for the neighborhood dead, and gardens provide vegetables and places to gather for home-grown performances. Visiting the Village becomes a ritual for our program, and the students' eyes widen as they turn each corner. On one side of the Village alley, there are houses bejeweled with mirrored faces and images of Ethiopian angels, and on the other, burned-out buildings. The squatters were just trying to keep warm when that one burned down.

The mosaic on the painted house, like the chalk drawings of children's homes in the school yard a few blocks away—all are images of a concrete urban makeover. The burned-out, beaten-up, sooted eye socket of a house, sinking into the rubble, faces the rehabbed, mosaic-mirrored eye,

and in reply,

it *winks.*

Figure 3.14 (Grade 4)

Figure 3.15 (Grade 4)

Interlude B

A conversation with David Howey, actor, who uses games as a training technique for learning Shakespeare.

David Howey:

"Yes *and*" is the key to improvisation. Never "no," never "block." Always open. A game helps you learn to be quick, to handle many things.

I would in class use actual playground games: "Red Rover," "Red Light, Green Light," "Grandmother's Footsteps," "Bringing Home the Bacon," "What Time Is It, Mr. Wolf?" You get, after this, physical alertness and an ability to change direction—mentally, physically—very quickly.

An exercise for Shakespeare preparation is "Snap, Clap, Chair"; you need immediate reaction without actors overthinking. Overthinking, overacting is always the danger. They have to learn there is a rhythm, which you need for Shakespeare. And if you break the rhythm . . .

There is the game "Ping Pong." Send "ping" around the circle clockwise, "pong" around the circle anticlockwise. You really have to focus and listen. . . . You're focusing. It gets people working together, with focus and fierce concentration.

We play with free association. Words are not only one meaning; there is sound, weight, syllabic length, connections. . . . That is exactly your engagement with the language when doing Shakespeare. When teachers are concerned with overinvolvement with words, you remove language. It helps you get what you want; the body and gestures fall into place.

There's the classic "What Are You Doing?" game. You have two people. One mimes an activity. What are you doing? Then the mimer lies. Then the next does what he says, and this one lies. To make it even more complicated, you can require that the sequence be alphabetical.

In my Shakespeare class, we move around the room and change direction with every punctuation mark. I teach they can change punctuation once they know how punctuation works. Why is that a period and not a colon? They are following a writer's roadmap, following script impulses when taught to only follow yourself.

I do physical exercises. Do a step on the last syllable of every line, changing lines, on every piece, skipping to the meter so you get the meter in the body, moving across the room on an idea change, banging one's fist on every emphasis. If they do the brainwork first, it gets in the way. We have to do the body first.

CHAPTER 4

Ball

School #6

Today my students and I pile into the van and head to the Bee Elementary School in Kensington, one of the poorest neighborhoods in the city. As we arrive, the six- and seven-year-olds are sitting on the concrete yard, patiently listening to visiting guests describe what they do. It is a SWAT team, complete with a machine gun and a Humvee. This is their enrichment program.

We are greeted by Mrs. Dee, an energetic and loving gym teacher. We are early, so she has us join her gym class. This class of seven-year-olds has some children with developmental delays, and she says that they are working on basic catching skills, so the balls we brought will be particularly useful. "Do we get to keep the tubs?" She grins when we tell her yes, the school can keep the materials and the tubs. Her eyebrows rise to the top of her curly hennaed hair when she sees what is inside. She picks up a sample of each toy and shows it to the children, who are sitting in rows on the small cramped gym floor. They ooh and aah, beaming sweet smiles. She quizzes them about what kinds of games one could play with each type of ball and appreciates that the footballs and tennis balls are in primary colors. This helps her as she organizes small teams by color.

Figure 4.1 (Grade 4)

Figure 4.2 (Grade 4)

Mrs. Dee firmly and patiently asks which child would like to play with each ball, and the children bounce their way outside, a flood in motion. Quickly they organize themselves into handball, dodgeball, and football catch. Shyer children bounce and catch tennis balls. Everyone moves. When they line up at the end of gym, their class teacher says with a smile, "Oh, you are having too much fun . . ." One little guy responds, "Oh, yes we *are!*"

Recess begins with a different set of classes. The activities continue, this time with basketballs added. Mrs. Dee has a girl take a boy to the sink because he has scraped his elbow. "You're his nurse; you take good care of him." And the girl gently guides him to the sink inside. The grown-ups retrieve a wayward ball from over the fence. The older girls bring out a boom box and search for the right spot for dancing. "Every day I dance with them." A boy asks if they can play two-handed touch football, and Mrs. Dee says, "Not today. You can only play a football game if I am steady quarterback." They acquiesce and play catch instead. Everything moves.

Figure 4.3 (Grade 4)

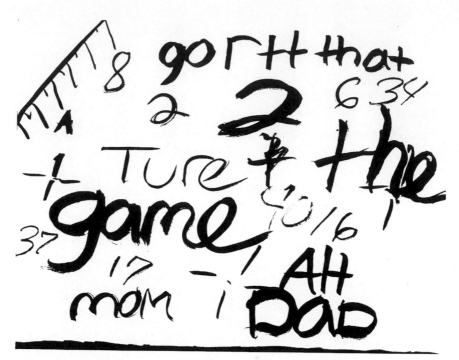

Figure 4.4 (Grade 4)

Figure 4.5 (Grade 4)

Figure 4.6 (Grade 4)

Mrs. Dee has so much to say. She disparages her "noonies," the non-teaching aides during the later lunch, who stand around and chat. "If you want the children to respect you, you have to play with them," she counsels. She said she had to fight to keep recess going, she and the school nurse. Mrs. Dee gladly takes the Recess Access brochures we carry to show to her staff, "in case they try to get rid of recess again." She notes that a kindergarten teacher who has a particularly challenging class is trying a new approach—her children get to move every two hours. She says it has made a world of difference and is shocked when I tell her that some schools have gotten rid of recess altogether. "The School District has a statement about health for each child. They're supposed to have recess. They have to move."

She happily tells us that this is the last year they will be in this build-ing, which seems to wheeze with age. The school serves eight hundred

Figure 4.7 (Grade 4)

Figure 4.8 (Grade 4)

children, some of whom meet in buildings a few blocks away. Next fall they will all be in a brand-new building, visible just past the burned-out factory. She says she will put up our new hoop there. She stares into my eyes, examining me. "Please come back in the fall," she says. She vows to have her second-graders write thank-you letters to us. I almost stop her but recognize that it seems to be important.

We ride back, wistful that this is the last trip this particular team of UARTS students will do together. They ask if they can help with the fall art activity, and I wish aloud that I could hire them all to do this project full time. I make up songs and sing all the way home.

School #7

The next crew of volunteers visits a neighborhood a few miles away at the Willie School, where City Year volunteers greet us and the office staff beams with appreciation. "Oh, the children are going to love this." Deirdre, a teaching aide, proudly gives us a tour of the school. Although it is rated a 1 out of 10 by Great Schools, it sparkles with the attention that a

Figure 4.9 (Grade 4)

caring staff provides. There are murals everywhere inside, in the stairwells and in the hallways, in the gym and outside the classrooms. The children's art is the freest we have seen yet: self-portraits in the style of Picasso, free-form paper cuts in the style of Matisse. Colonially dressed wooden-spoon dolls share a display case with tribal masks, a thought-provoking juxta-position. There is real art here, and I ask Deirdre if she can take us to the art teacher. I want to shake her hand. Ms. Mary is humble and gives the children all the credit. When we move outside, I offer to return with art supplies in the fall, and she cheerfully smiles her appreciation and is eager to collaborate.

At Willie, the kindergartners through the sixth grade get a recess after lunch. As in many schools, gym and art are once a week for everyone. Four classes are usually outside in the concrete yard at once. Today we get to see the first-graders, six- and seven-year-olds, and my students are as excited as the children. We bring out two of the buckets and leave the hoop and basketballs inside. Through the window I watch the children standing around with nothing to play

Figure 4.10 (Grade 4)

Figure 4.11 (Grade 4)

with. Then we emerge. Ms. Smith, the aide, shouts, "It's Christmas in June! Christmas in June!" The children realize the materials are for them, and they shout and pour over the buckets like liquid, stragglers zooming in like bees to honey. There is an explosion of movement, and in a few minutes the yard is a festival of activity. Jump rope, wall ball, football, catch, and dozens of children just bouncing and catching, bouncing and catching. The aide says, "I've been here nineteen years and I've never seen them look so happy."

The colorful tennis balls manage to roll under the fence into the street, and I spend my time gathering them and tossing them back to the children in waves. I get a good workout, scooping and lobbing balls that have minds of their own. One boy holds out his hand for me to pass a ball to him, putting his small hand through the fence like something out of prison movie. When I pass it to him, he gives me a pumpkin-toothed smile that seems wider than his whole face.

Shy, slim Mr. Martinez, an aide of grandfather age, is also getting a workout retrieving tennis balls from the street. I worry that the staff will

Figure 4.12 (Grade 4)

Figure 4.13 (Grade 4)

be angry with us because we donated a bucketful of these bouncy tennis balls in bright primary colors. But the staff members are giddy with pleasure and decide to move the small-ball activity to a more protected corner, reducing the rolling in odd directions. When Mr. Martinez hands a ball back to one last child and asks him to replace it in the bucket, the child replies with a huge hug, and it is clear that the staff is enjoying the new materials almost as much as the children. They have the children chorus their "thank you" when recess is over.

The chalk is scattered and ferociously used, and I vow to bring more when I return in the fall. Ms. Smith gathers her children and kisses her fingertips and blows them toward us. "Much love, much love." We are awed by the energy released.

Figure 4.14 (Grade 4)

Figure 4.15 (Grade 4)

It has been a rough week for them, I hear. One child was killed last week, playing on a train track when he touched a live wire. His brother is at the school, and there are memorials in every corridor. There will be a talent show in the child's honor. I silently dedicate these playthings to his memory.

Two years later: I park my beat-up van in front of the Willie School again. This is the third time in two weeks that I've gone to this school in Northeast Philadelphia and waited for recess. I hear raucous play sounds, but it is from the Catholic school across the street. The Willie school yard is silent again. Ms. Mary, the inspirational art teacher and master artist, is gone. Owing to budget cuts, she has not been replaced.

Two girls linger by a window with their backpacks on as they move to their next class. They face the yard for a moment and droop as if they need watering. Their teacher calls to them to move along. When I phone the office to ask if the children will have recess today, the answer is "Not today. Not every day." When I ask why, there is silence. I ask, is it because of punishment? No, the secretary offers and then pauses. Is it for enrichment? Yes, yes, that's it. Enrichment. A car blasts angry poetry as I leave.

Figure 4.16 (Grade 4)

Figure 4.17 (Grade 4)

Figure 4.18 (Grade 4)

The Bee School in Kensington has moved since my last visit, so I pull my van over to ask a school crossing guard for directions. She is in uniform, talking to two men sitting on the ground on her corner who are drinking from brown-bagged beer bottles. None of them has a full set of front teeth. She's heard of the school, heard of the street it is on, but has no idea where it is. She sends me to the next crossing guard three blocks away. "She'll know. She drives."

The next crossing guard is talking affectionately with a young woman, most likely a relative by the shape of their faces. The two women greet me kindly and let me know that the school I seek is a few lights away. The crossing guard calls me "Hon" and tells me to close my window and lock my car doors as I drive. She believes that I am not safe in my own car. The only building that is maintained en route is "Safeguard Self Storage." The people look shabby, but their stuff is safe. Unemployment is visibly higher here, and each block hosts men from their twenties to their forties, sitting, drinking, or leaning on windowless buildings. Access to medical care and dental care is scarce here, missing front teeth the norm.

Figure 4.19 (Grade 4)

Figure 4.20 (Grade 4)

The school emerges, a brand-new building with a small yard on one side with divisions painted to indicate where classes are to gather. The opposite side has a fenced-in yard. There are no hoops, but one class has the whole yard to itself with plenty of play materials. There are at least eight balls of varying sizes, at least six hula hoops, and a large handful of jump ropes. It appears that there is a toy for every three children. The children look relaxed, light in spirit as they busily bounce and dribble and jump and sway, and I cheer Mrs. Dee and her determination. The children practice ball passing and running, ball passing and running, passing and running.

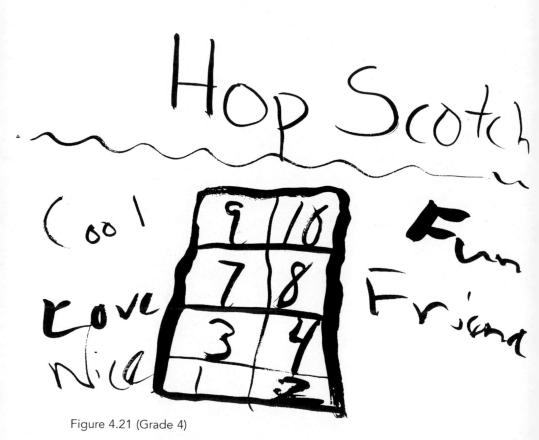

Figure 4.21 (Grade 4)

Figure 4.22 (Grade 4)

Megan LaMon

Interlude C

Conversations with Ron Kerber and Evan Solot, jazz musicians. Although both perform and compose, one is known for his playful improvisations in performance, the other for playful arrangements. They describe their forms of practice and the parallels in music, games, and poetry.

Ron Kerber:

It is still about finding the jokes, the wit, finding the joke when I write that makes me laugh when I compose. Much of it is about relationships. We are solitary, like a painter, when we practice. Then we do get to the "playground"—I have a great deal of joy when playing with others.

One of the things that's different for a freshman [musician], you practice how to practice. You have to learn how to get out of the way so you can play. When you are practicing all the time, when you play, you have to forget about it, so you can have a relationship with the bass player. You have to forget the self.

The more I knew, the less playful I was. My father played the trumpet; he talked about "soul." He was a larger-than-life figure, an engineer who wrote music all night. He used to talk about how "you have to get lost." We knew what he meant.

Today, when I improvise, I have to close my eyes, go to another place. There, there's no spotlight, no sound of cash registers, getting lost in sound and emotion. I think we're missing the boat. We have to strip all that away in pedagogy and get them to be six again. They're so stuck in the academic world of skills. They forget how to play.

Anna Beresin:

You close your eyes?

Ron Kerber:

It's nonverbal, nonvisual. It's emotional. If you're figuring out how to end a tune, you can see it with exaggerated gestures or you can feel it. It's aural. Go ask Stevie Wonder. If I've played with someone on a regular basis, I can see his mood. I can be sympathetic. If he's not giving me a lot of room, I'll let him have the ball. He needs to shoot more. Sometimes it's so powerful, you just met someone five minutes earlier and you immediately feel that connection. You're going to really know each other for the next several hours.

There's more fear in composing for me. I would say I'm more of a performer than a composer. When performing, you can feel the response immediately.

When I'm writing music at my best, I don't care what anyone else thinks. When I'm at my best, I don't care. This is art. Entertainment is about caring about the audience first. As a performer, I can feel immediately if something is good or bad, although it doesn't mean I am going to change it.

With the creative process, the more time you have to think, second-guess it, the less playful you are. As a composer, you have a lot of time to question. As a performer, you're in the moment. That can feel intimidating to some people. To me it's okay; I'll be able to feel if it's okay.

At times you're a point guard. You might be a bass player; there are rules and guidelines. But there's all this freedom in basketball. Pro ball has a lot of freedom. The 76ers, they've really bought in to each other. It's a good band, as opposed to a bunch of soloists.

Practicing, like Catholics saying the rosary, practicing is a ritual. It is an entrance, a way in. When you think of the three elements of music—rhythm, melody, harmony—my father had the one that overlapped all of that: emotion. Men tend to be uncomfortable being emotional. If we weren't playing from the heart, we weren't tapping into the most emotional pieces. If you don't learn how to play, how to get in touch with feelings, you can't really teach it.

I think the very notion of D minor 7 flat 5, G 7 sharp 9 to a C minor major 7 is the progression thousands of people use over and over. What makes it different for each of is the adjectives and adverbs we use.

The sound of surprise. In my office I have a poster: "Jazz. The Sound of Surprise." You want to be surprised. You want to be tickled.

Evan Solot:

There is a lot of play in composing because you're moving stuff around, whether in my head, at a computer, at a keyboard.

Technically, it is "playing around," but I'm not thinking "play." If it's play, it's painful play, like childbirth. It was play when you finished, not when you're in it, when it's really tough. Like a crossword, jigsaw puzzle. The "eureka" moments are great, but few and far between. When you're doing it for a long time, it's a craft; I hesitate to call it art. When there's a deadline, it's very satisfying. When there's no deadline, then it gets hard. I feel responsible for it.

There was a time when I was doing theater, teaching, having a family; I was complaining that I didn't have enough time. My wife suggested I get up early. I was desperate, so I'd set my alarm for 5. After having coffee, dealing with the dogs, I'd write from 5:30 a.m. to 7 a.m. [*Rolls eyes.*] At that hour of the a.m., the critic is still asleep, the one who sits on my shoulder and laughs at everything. G-sharp? Ha!

Most of the time that was pretty good. If you do that five to six days a week, that's a whole day. I tell my students to embrace the fact that we obsess. One technique I have is not allowing myself to work on the same project two days in a row. Composing is improvisation, but you have an eraser at the end of it.

Anna Beresin:

What's the difference between doing a puzzle and composing?

Evan Solot:

I sit down and I start the piece from the beginning and try to sit back and listen to it. When you write two notes, sometimes it tells you what the third note wants to be. My teacher said you have to have a reason for every note you do. Then after a while, he told me to stop doing that.

I build things that sound like improvisation. When working with poet Franz Wright, his poem "The Hawk" begins, "Maybe in a million years . . ." and I wanted to play with all the "maybes" and "perhaps." In the beginning the voices all sing "maybe" with different times, different speeds, but written that way, sometimes on the same note, or up a half-step, down a half-step. Another spot, two tempos exist at the same time, like a cross-fade.

Without a deadline, I spend too much time. I have another trick, to not work linearly. I'll write the ending, I'll write the middle, and figure it out. That's a better way. You know, set it up like a mystery, ending with "The butler did it," and how to make that arc. When I asked Franz Wright about the hawk poem, he said, "Which one? I've written that poem thirty or forty times."

The collaboration is a playtime—you throw things out and see how someone responds. Who is searching for what to run with. You're gauging response, as opposed to solitary creation, where response is your imagination.

I'm so lucky. I'm doing R & B, classical, jazz, dance, theater, different categories of music, different deadlines. Every one of them is work, is fun, and is play. There is that feeling of delight when an idea works—either because that spot has a potential solution and/or that it's leading me into new possibilities.

It's temporary, of course, because even if I embrace it, I quickly take it for granted and begin to wrestle with the new situation it presents.

CHAPTER 5

Rope

School #8

As we drive to the Rodriguez School in East Central Philadelphia, we wind our way through one-way streets, past burned-out factories. The school pops up like a cactus flower among the rubble. A bright and open facility, it serves eight hundred students, the vast majority Spanish-speaking.

Ms. Gale, an administrator, greets us enthusiastically and arranges to have several classes play before their lunch, even though they usually play afterward. She has us lay out all the recess toys and invites the children to inspect them. They look at the material with curiosity, and the grins emerge when they realize it is for them and they will get to play with it soon. One girl eyes the jump ropes. "We haven't had jump ropes since 2008." That was two years ago.

The jump ropes fly out of the buckets and lead to lots of jumping practice. The children use the ropes for making impromptu trains, for linking friends, for swinging low to the ground for classmates to jump over. The ropes are used more for theater props than jumping, and I realize how alien they must seem to the children. But then they gingerly start to com-

Figure 5.1 (Grade 3)

Figure 5.2 (Grade 3)

plicate their jumping. "Cinderella," they sing. I sing, "Dressed in yella," and their eyes widen: "How did she know that?"

The teachers ask our students to explain their majors. One fifth-grade girl eyes our student's camera. "How do I get to be a photographer?" Our student explains that you begin by taking pictures and that even an inexpensive camera can lead to beautiful images. Then the floodgates open and the balls start being used: wall ball, basketball, football, catch, bouncing, tossing, lobbing, and rolling.

They draw hopscotches, and they are not playing with them but just drawing them. A male staffer offers to get a ladder to put up the basketball hoops. They have only two hoops, and they have to take them down each day so the neighborhood kids don't destroy them after school. The staff bustle, the children hustle, and our students are invited in.

Ms. Gale, a pale, gentle woman, comments that one of the children drawing with our film major has cancer. She murmurs, "You have to let kids be kids" and doles out hugs every two minutes to children of

Figure 5.3 (Grade 3)

Figure 5.4 (Grade 3)

different sizes. When she first took this job, she was told to expect the worst. But children are children, and she fell in love, despite some early challenges with violence. At the end of her first year, one tough little boy said, "I bet you're not coming back." When she returned the next fall, the children accepted her as their own. Now she has no intention of leaving.

Her colleague, Ms. Jones, appreciates the donation and wishes they had "one of those programs where grown-ups come and teach the children how to play." I point out to her that the yard is filled with playing children, and her eyes widen. She sees my point that children need stimulation, and not necessarily instruction. I consider it a small victory.

The principal asks if the students can come back for career day. They agree to, and I offer to return with art supplies in the fall. Her kind face

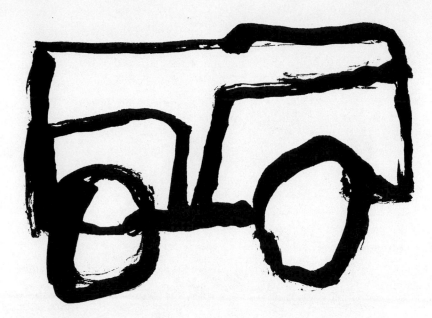

Figure 5.5 (Grade 3)

Figure 5.6 (Grade 3)

blushes with excitement, and we shake hands to seal our promise of return. The one child's line echoes in my ears: "We haven't had jump ropes since 2008." When you are ten years old, that space of two years is one-fifth of your life, a third of your middle childhood, the equivalent of decades in adult years.

Extra Lengths

When we return months later to donate art materials, we watch the children at play before the art class, warmly nostalgic as our bright green Recess Access buckets are brought out and swarmed. The boys are let out first, leaving the girls few materials, but they make do, and girls pull lines of classmates cheerily attached by one long rope. Dozens of children are running and laughing. As we pass by a younger class near the small built plastic climbing apparatus in a side section of the school yard, the children wait in line for a turn to move, reminding me that loose parts on a playground provide greater opportunities for play.

In order not to miss out, the art teacher crams two classes in a classroom built for one. Forty-five second-graders get yelled at as they come in. Their paintings are exuberant as they fondly remember our gift of new balls, ropes, and hoops. Two girls bathe their black hands in the

Figure 5.7 (Grade 3)

Figure 5.8 (Grade 3)

India ink. One boy sneaks a painted mustache and beard on himself. When their classroom teacher picks them up, she informs the art teacher that "their time to go to the bathroom was two and a half hours ago and therefore they do not have time to wash." One boy who spilled a whole dish of ink on his khaki uniform is crying, as he fears punishment. It seems he did the same thing last week. The teacher consoles him and I help him to clean his uniform. When we leave, the kind principal assures me that she has extras and insists that it comes out of her budget. The children each paint at least three paintings, some even more, and the teacher goes on and on about the significance of our copy paper donation. They have almost run out of paper in the art room, and it is only October.

I return several times more, to give back their paintings, to show the principal the photographs. Each time, we are greeted with hugs and extended handshakes. The materials are still in use, the principal assures us, the yard an oasis among abandoned factories.

Figure 5.9 (Grade 3)

Figure 5.10 (Grade 3)

Figure 5.11 (Grade 3)

Figure 5.12 (Grade 3)

Megan LaMon

Interlude D

A conversation with Brian Sanders, modern dance choreographer, known for his playful use of materials.
I explain to Brian Sanders that I study playgrounds.
He responds:

I study playgrounds, too. I study the architecture, for sliding, swinging, climbing. I am always looking for new props. I've even had rehearsals on playgrounds.

Every time I start a project, it's literally about play, jumping into a project and playing. The artists that work for me have to be playful. I find it interesting, finding stuff that works comes from play.

That's part of my torture as an artist. Dance is fundamentally an expression of joy. Strange thing about art is how to be playful and serious at the same time; it is torturous.

A lot of my work comes from found objects. First, we play with the found object, exploring its potential for movement, its image. A big part of play is exploring. In this new piece I'm doing, one Egyptian gesture [symbolically] compresses two thousand years of history. What is our one hundred years going to be compressed into?

We've collided hip-hop and Lindy Hop, geishas and voguing, Rockettes and goose steps.

I wanted to bring the innocence of children and children's games into pieces, and I bumped up against a wall. I think I need to play as an adult. I imagine the skills are the same. I love some of the old playgrounds, monkey bars, and unconquerable, infinite possibility. The need to hang, to slide. I am an apparatus person; I need to navigate from one to the next.

There's this balance between play and play with purpose. I play with purpose too much. I keep finding new playgrounds. Last summer I started doing Rollerblades, this year snowboarding. When I feel blocked, I go toward reading other artists, go back to play, to go back to the creative spirit.

My latest play is with technology. But it doesn't expand. It goes in, to a narrowing point. It doesn't do what getting on a playground does. The more creative the playground [structure], the harder it is to create; it's already done.

Who wouldn't want to play in a closet?

Who wouldn't want to climb on a Calder?

PART III

Megan LaMon

Balancing Acts

CHAPTER 6

"We Invented It"/
"We Taught Them"

"What Time Is It, Mr. Fox?" I taught them that game.
—MR. SMYTHE, GYM TEACHER

We invented it.
—JULIE, AGE 10

The Carlyle School has the most kinetic school yard I have seen in this city, with children climbing, jumping rope, playing kickball and basketball—a stark contrast to the eight other Philadelphia schools, where initially no child had access to playground props and where we recorded comments such as "Our playground balls were stolen three years ago and were never replaced"; "We haven't had any jump ropes since 2008"; "Our school does not allow recess." This school yard is different, with an active parent group and a young, energetic principal. No one at this upper-middle-class school is stating the recurring motif of our working-class, materially deprived schools, the falsehood that "children just don't know how to play."

The plan here was to embed a small quantitative study within a larger qualitative study of play. Usually that is done the other way around. Beyond the cultural, social, and psychological importance of recess, what could be proven about recess's unique offering to the bodies of schoolchildren? Because gym class serves as a substitute for recess in many schools, how do children move at recess as compared with physical education classes? How does recess serve children physically, and can it be considered an overlooked, inexpensive, child-led, anti-obesity program?

The research team monitored the number of steps taken in both recess and gym class through the use of pedometers, small digital watch-like devices that count the steps one takes. Although pedometers technically can also calculate calories burned, we decided, given the differences in movement quality, exertion, and stride length per step, to focus exclusively on step count. This way the step count per minute of one activity can be compared with the step count per minute of another. The question was whether we could prove that recess offered the equivalent step count, and implied burning of calories, as gym.

"Mine's gonna say a million bajillion." So says Kenya, an energetic nine-year-old who eagerly puts on a pedometer. "What's the highest score? Was it Sam?" asks the gym teacher. For two weeks in the spring of 2011, we recorded the pedometer count from all available physical activities for nine-year-olds from beginning to end. During gym, all the activity was directed by one teacher. The gym teachers at this school also supervised lunch recess with walkie-talkies and presented stern personas with soft underbellies. They too were excited about the pedometers and had the children do their most vigorous activities in gym class.

Figure 6.1 (Grade 3)

Figure 6.2 (Grade 3)

Figure 6.3 (Grade 3)

As in many upper-middle-class schools, children in this school often missed movement because it was replaced by enrichment activities such as chorus, library, technology, and counseling. And as in many Philadelphia working-class schools, children here also missed movement as a punishment. One could say that it is a multiclassed school, since recess was being increasingly squeezed for both enrichment and punishment purposes.

Letters of invitation to participate in the study were sent to all the children's families explaining the study's purpose, noting that the school and children would be de-identified and that the whole school would receive materials as a thank-you gift.[1] Although dozens wished to participate, only twelve returned the parent-and-child permission slips, five boys and seven girls. The children wearing pedometers played as they would normally play with their usual friends, for twenty minutes after each lunch. They performed the same activities as the other children and enacted their normal everyday routines. The three aides who assisted the teachers at recess were appreciative of the donation. Three of their balls had popped only that week, and there was no money in the budget to replace them.

Figure 6.4 (Grade 3)

Figure 6.5 (Grade 3)

The pedometers were ordered from a well-respected supplier of educational fitness materials.[2] At the end of each play period, the pedometer and belt were collected, the times noted, and the steps recorded. Before the research began, the pedometers were tested for sensitivity. There were three possible settings for pedometer sensitivity, and our research staff concurred that the middle setting accurately counted steps when a variety of movements were performed. All pedometers were set to this same level of step sensitivity and monitored daily for setting consistency. Because the same children wore the pedometers in both gym and recess, whatever inconsistencies occurred in the instrument were consistent for that child. In other words, the relative number of steps taken per minute was comparable.

The step count was not easily visible to the children because it was hidden by the pedometer's plastic cover, although the children were aware that the pedometer counted steps. At the end of each period of data col-

Figure 6.6 (Grade 3)

TABLE 6.1. TALLIES OF AVERAGE STEPS TAKEN BY 12 CHILDREN

LOCATION	Outdoor Recess	Indoor Recess	Gym (Whole)	Gym (Half)
DURATION	20 min.	20 min.	40 min.	20 min.
Day 1	1562		1753	876
Day 2		1348		
Day 3	1147		1436	718
Day 4	954			
Day 5	910			
Day 6	1171			
TOTAL AVG	1149	1348	1595	797
STEPS PER MINUTE	60	67	40	38

lection, if children asked for their step count, the information was shared. It was observed that some children who were concerned with step count were equally aware of the pedometer's presence in play and in gym class. Most of the children ignored the pedometer's presence and simply went about their activities.

Gym is a once-a-week class and served as the pedometer baseline. The entire study occurred over a two-week span: two groups of children in two gym classes were studied, and a total of six days of recess, three per week. Additional time was spent observing at the school over the course of a month and talking with children, teachers, and nonteaching staff. The hypothesis was that free play was at least as aerobic as organized gym, and more diverse in activity. The surprise, when the findings were considered, was the magnitude in the difference between recess and gym.

The average free play session at recess offered 30 percent more steps per minute than gym. Ironically, this was true even when the gym teacher offered half the gym period as a choice activity. Indoor recess offered an even more dramatic finding of 67 steps per minute, as contrasted with 38 steps per minute of adult-led activity (Table 6.1). The results are highly statistically significant.[3]

How to explain this? Much of the gym time was spent waiting or observing other children doing an activity. Many of the children seemed

Figure 6.7 (Grade 3)

Figure 6.8 (Grade 3)

to enjoy the organized gym games, which ranged from running to yokum volleyball to basketball, although there was typically only one activity going at a time. The gym teachers were as eager to impress our research team with their most active repertoire as the children were to show us their favorite games. Some children played the same game in gym as they did in recess. But in gym, there were several children who would slink to the back, choosing not to participate. Gym games were always organized by the adults. If there were simultaneous activities, they were in parallel with each other. In contrast, on the playground the children linked their moves to the activities and transitioned themselves physically, creating a collage of movement.

Play as Invention

"Who wants to play foursquare?" "Me! Me! Me!" "Out!" "Foul!" As these were shouted, a smaller, dreamy-eyed child wandered by singing, "Miss Mary M, M, M, all dressed in MILK, MILK, MILK." Children stepped in and out of play in the school yard, offering tokens of friendship wrapped in bits of culture. Claire, a frail pale girl, positioned her orange Tic Tac candy as a "gold tooth" in the space where her baby tooth had fallen out. "Look at me, I'm Lil Wayne."

The most subdued of the children in our study, Claire announced that she does not eat lunch at all, "'cause of my ADHD medication." She moved the least (628 steps compared with a group average of 1194), and I wondered whether the medication robbed her and her slower classmates of their energy to move. Claire stepped an average of 628 times at recess and averaged only 269 steps in gym.

For some athletic children like Sam and Mary, gym and recess offered another beloved opportunity to play kickball or basketball. The ones who sought other ways of expressing themselves seemed to benefit most from recess time. Some, like Ana, needed to sprint and then sit, sprint and sit. Others, like Kim, preferred twirling and making themselves dizzy. Mario enjoyed organizing wall ball, and Julie liked to rule foursquare. What they had in common was their passion, their intensity, and, apparently, the number of steps they take as they play. Some children were more active than others, but there were no clear patterns by gender.[4]

TABLE 6.2. AVERAGE STEPS PER MINUTE (SPM) PER CHILD

	Recess Avg. for 20 Min.	Recess Indoor Avg. for 20 Min.	Gym 20 Min.
PSEUDONYM			
Jordan	685	X	400
Sam	1249	1223	950
Claire	628	733	269
Michael	850	1343	600
Rashawn	1276	1706	722
Kim	1491	1603	511
Kenya	1143	1060	745
Ana	1292	912	924
Mary	1164	1659	1000
Rayna	1275	X	X
Mario	1630	1891	1228
Julie	1647	X	1078
AVERAGE SPM	1194	1348	766

Note: X = data unavailable.

"What TIME is it, Mr. Fox?" "2:00!" and the line of children asking took two steps closer to the child in charge. "What TIME is it, Mr. Fox?" "5:00!" and they took five steps closer to the child in charge. "What TIME is it, Mr. Fox?" "Midnight!" and the children scattered, running all over the concrete playground. But unlike in gym, where they first learned the game, in the school yard they ran in a scattered formation, hiding, dancing, tripping, and slipping into new games. Across the yard, three children worked hard to get a stuck basketball out of the hoop, throwing their shoes, lunchboxes, and other projectiles to eventually free it, and then cheered their victory. A serious game of kickball involving twenty children was played next to the hoop, adjacent to a half-dozen children playing "suicide handball," which quietly mixed with wall ball and tag. The activities on the playground were superimposed with varying interactions and overlapping rhythms, echoing the city itself with its sirens, car alarms, trucks idling, and shouts for attention.

In many of the cases, twenty minutes of recess offered several hundred steps more per child than the equivalent gym class (see Table 6.2).

Figure 6.9 (Grade 3)

For Claire and Kim, it was more than double (628 vs. 269; 1491 vs. 511). For Sam and Mary, the difference between recess and gym was slight. Indoor recess was more kinetic than outdoor, and we hypothesize that this had something to do with the crowding effect, as well as the fact that the sound echoed the intensity of so many bodies in an indoor space. But the staff lamented the overcrowding and perceived indoor recess as over-stimulating and potentially dangerous. In other Philadelphia schools, inclement weather brings the total cancelation of any kind of movement or play.[5]

Recess, with its playtime, is clearly not the same as adult organized physical education. Australian folklorist June Factor quotes a child who wisely counsels, "It is not play if you can't choose."[6] The children show us that play is more than a general choice of activity. Play is about a host of choices, a variety of invented moves. Recess offers time to play with the variables of the body and of culture.

Figure 6.10 (Grade 3)

Figure 6.11 (Grade 3)

Variables at Play

During play, as in dance, movement varies among several sets of polarities. Using dancers' vocabulary to describe movement, let us examine school-yard play with choreographer Rudolf Laban's terms of "effort" and "shape."[7] Laban divided all movement into the motion factors of space, time, weight, and flow. Spatially, each body part and the body as a whole can move in a way that is "direct" or "indirect." Time can be "sudden" or "sustained." Weight can be "strength" or "lightness." The flow can be "free" or "bound." This means that a child can change the quality of the motion, for each body part, and its duration and intensity. The movement shape of the body part or of the whole body can be opening or closing and in relation to the movement of other bodies or objects and the environment. This means that a child can change the shape of his or her own body expressively and adjust to the movement of everything else going on around it.

In addition, at play, one can vary the volume, pitch, and timber of sound; the choice of words, both direct and indirect in meaning; and the choice of props, of play partners, of audience, of privacy, and of rela-

Figure 6.12 (Grade 3)

Figure 6.13 (Grade 3)

tive location to and touching of nonpartners. Movers can play with their immediate body space, their general direction, and the observed shape that emerges from each body part. Each mover moves in relationship to other movers and in relationship to objects and the built environment.

Laban's language suggests that the key variable distinguishing gym from free play is the degree of directness or indirectness in each movement. On the playground, as described, the children can focus on an end point or allow themselves to meander, to experience chance encounters with other children, to open themselves up to possibilities. There is no agenda in the school yard, although children may choose to create their own agendas. As Laban himself wrote, "Dance is stylized play."[8]

Play, as opposed to physical education instruction, can be considered a type of "exaggerated negotiated movement." The children move in and around each other, reading each other's cues as they holler their intentions. The social challenge of all play is in the negotiation of play's indi-

Figure 6.14 (Grade 3)

rectness. Katie Salen and Eric Zimmerman, known for their scholarship of game design, define play as "free movement within a more rigid structure."[9] But this free movement is necessarily negotiated, even if one is playing alone. Several decades earlier, psychologist Erik Erikson wrote that play gives the illusion of excess space and time.[10] For Jean Piaget, play offers a host of moral adjustments, suggesting that with freedom comes not just physical movement but a practice of mental movement.[11] For Lev S. Vygotsky and for Donald W. Winnicott, it is this in-between zone of play that allows for growth; we develop through play precisely because it allows for vacillating motion.[12] For Sutton-Smith, play is defined by its ambiguity; it is a layered form of communication that is intentionally vague.[13] This is perhaps the key distinction between gym and recess: the relative amount of openness, indirectness, and exaggeration in group movement.

The indirectness or exaggeration of play is typically eliminated by grown-ups in gym classes. Teams are decided for the children. The order of players is decided for the children. The order of activities and their location are decided for the children. The use of props is decided for the

Figure 6.15 (Grade 3)

children. The songs they chant are decided for the children. The duration of time of each activity is decided for the children. Whereas outside, in recess, you hear, "Spit, spit, you are not it," with toes and hands in motion as the children count out who will begin and who will be "it." There is no lag time spent waiting once "it" is chosen, no need to sit and wait for adults to reframe the rules.

It can be said that play parallels the grown-up jobs in a given culture, and that as adult life has become more sedentary and directed, so children's lives are more sedentary and directed.[14] The decrease in jobs that include physical labor and the increase in car ownership with longer commutes to employment have reduced our overall cultural movement vocabulary.

Childhood obesity is now epidemic in Philadelphia. In 2010, 50 percent of Philadelphia's children 6–12 years old were overweight or obese, according to a public health survey, and pediatricians are now seeing ailments associated with obesity and aging among the very young.[15] Junk

Figure 6.16 (Grade 3)

food aside, children in the city move less than their parents did. The reasons include the decrease in the number of children walking to school, the decrease in the number of children allowed to play outside after school, changing toy selection due to the power of marketing, and the reduction of recess or playtime in the school day itself. Clearly, physical education is important, and movement time is more essential than ever. This book suggests a symbiotic relationship between gym and recess, but at recess, children move more, say more, and have a chance to encounter a wider range of novel experiences.

CHAPTER 7

The Paintlore of Children

Look at them, looking . . .
—WILLIAM CARLOS WILLIAMS
TO ROBERT COLES, 1992, 1

I n all the paintings of Recess Access, grown-ups are never visible in the school yard, but they are occasionally written to or presented as voices or icons.[1] One fourth-grader whose class had lost its recess painted, "I have my eye on you," with a large eyeball taking up the whole frame (see Figure 4.18). The children watch the grown-ups watching them, and then go ahead and play, in a world made up of children with children, framed by adults.

What these paintings "mean" is complex, perhaps unknowable. Yet they certainly portray a set of truths, truths about activity preference, about friendship wishes, truths of mood, truths of imagination, and truths of repression. The types of games portrayed are historical facts. The observation that individual portraiture disappeared in fifth grade is a psychological one. That cultural icons from Hello Kitty to Justin Bieber emerged in fourth grade is a cultural one. That second-graders typically drew images of themselves, third-graders of pairs, and fifth-graders of large groups a particularly interesting sociological one. They can be seen as pieces of ethnographic truth, or the framing of historical time and place around childhood, props, and movement. In order to make sense

Figure 7.1 (Grade 2)

of all this, we need to balance lenses from psychology, anthropology, and folklore in addition to the perspectives of the children.

The children painted as much or as little as they wanted to within a class period. Some made multiple paintings. The images, then, are not a sample proportionally reflecting the grade but rather a set of visual stories that emerged from within a cohort. More than a hundred children painted, and each time, they experimented appreciatively with the new brushes, asking for more paper, more paper. They allowed me to view their play worlds from the edge of their playgrounds, but they allowed me to enter through their paintings.

Figure 7.2 (Grade 2)

Early audiences for these pictures noted the relative simplicity in all the paintings and the fact that many of the paintings of the ten-year-olds are technically similar to the paintings of the seven-year-olds.[2] Many children had rarely held a paintbrush, and unlike art in most art programs, these paintings were done in one sitting. Yet the brush lines indicate emotion; proportion suggests concepts, placement, intention.[3]

Figure 7.3 (Grade 2)

After one class of children showed me their football paintings and jump-rope images, many with the dark rain clouds of the day, I asked them how it felt to use the brushes. Stephan, a boy with wide brown eyes, offered, "Delicious," and said it slowly, softly, like a confession. Tyree, who seemed to have a permanently perplexed expression, gestured with his hands and muttered, "Smooth." Yet another lamented that their regu-

Figure 7.4 (Grade 2)

Figure 7.5 (Grade 2)

lar brushes are all hard and stiff. A particularly small girl, Mia, said that they had not had "real brushes since 2008." Again, this reflected a two-year gap. Tyree announced, "You can really paint your feelings with these brushes."

Robert Coles's trilogy—*The Moral Life of Children, The Political Life of Children,* and *The Spiritual Life of Children*—used children's art as a storytelling device and inspired the design of this project. For Coles, children's art is embedded in a larger psychological narrative of our collective humanism, addressing social injustices, theological wrestlings, the emotions of political strife. These all emerge as literal centerpieces in his larger tale of culturally stylized identity struggle.

Before Coles, Donald W. Winnicott used drawings to understand the messages embedded in children's play as therapeutic storytelling. Before Winnicott, Erik Erikson would show images to children as a way to share concepts too complicated for words. The body itself is a sculpture for Erikson, and pain is a clue to stories within. Anna Freud compared children's paintings to dreams, as her father did with play and creative writing. The fields of art therapy and play therapy overlap in this manner, and both employ these symbolic tools as ways to get into the individual child's head.[4]

Although given an invitation to follow children's cultures, Coles was more interested in children's places in the adult world. In the transcript of one conversation with a Nicaraguan child, he asks, "Do you always like what you hear the Sandinistas say? Does your mother like what she hears? Your father, does he go to the rallies?" The reply is "I don't follow all the speeches. Maybe I watch the people too much, so I don't hear the words coming from the platform! I'm trying to see which of my friends is there, so we can play!"[5]

We do not get to read what they actually played. Coles's novel idea was to utilize children's art as a social science tool, an alternative affective method of understanding children's hearts, as he began to analyze his massive collection: "As I look at several hundred drawings by South Africa's colored children, I begin to realize that this is one of the moments in my research when I feel strangely categorical, when the social-science phrase that usually bothers me, 'a finding,' begins to come to mind."[6]

At the same time, he analyzed specific drawings, the way an art historian might, paying attention to form and composition, to cultural

Figure 7.6 (Grade 2)

Figure 7.7 (Grade 2)

references, and to what was perhaps not drawn. In *The Spiritual Life of Children,* he describes the phrases accompanying the drawing, the drawings themselves, and the sheer quantity of his collection: "If I may be statistical: I have accumulated 293 pictures of God; all but 38 are pictures of His face, with maybe a neck, some shoulders, but no torso, arms or legs."[7]

More recently, Lisa Mitchell, an anthropologist, wrote about the need to think critically about using children's drawings as a visual research method, noting, "Children's drawings have gained renewed interest as anthropologists and other researchers search for methods that align with the current conceptualization of children as social agents and cultural producers."[8] Mitchell cautions against speaking for children

Figure 7.8 (Grade 2)

Figure 7.9 (Grade 2)

and notes that children vary individually and culturally in the way they choose to verbalize or not verbalize their thoughts. They may draw what is expected of them, and yet drawing allows for the opening of taboo topics.[9]

The 155 paintings of recess and their corresponding lore are urban paintings, Philadelphia paintings, with slight variations by neighborhood. In one school the children thought the large buildings viewed outside their classroom window were the skyscrapers of New York City. They had never traveled the few miles to Philadelphia's city center, and they associated skyscrapers with famous images they had seen on television. In the poorest of Philadelphia neighborhoods, there were more paintings of breakfast and food. There were more images of angry children and angry brush strokes at schools where recess had been removed as a punishment. One could say the paintings are an urban summary of icons, portraits, and verbs.[10]

Perhaps the most influential of developmental psychologists, Jean Piaget saw the child as a scientist, experimenting at play with gravity, with space, with number, and with democracy.[11] He, too, had children draw, although the context of the paintings was not his main interest;

rather, he saw art, games, and mathematical errors as entranceways into the minds of individual children within an age cohort. Piaget was a fan of John Dewey's, and both men felt that children need to experience creation themselves, to physically move materials in order to practice thinking.[12]

This collection of paintings suggests that children reach beyond experimentation, beyond science, and step into art and cultural variation through indirect group practice. The vast majority of the paintings show a world of childhood in which children practice stylized motion, with an increasing use of props and an increasing number of playmates as the children get older. Younger ones paint more images of the lone child (13/29), slightly older ones often draw twosomes, and the oldest children typically include whole groups of children (22/41), reflecting the increasing complexity of the school-age child's social and creative worlds. Their complexity increases, as well as their expertise in specific cultural styles and the range of their cultural vocabulary.

The fifth-graders' paintings demonstrate their knowledge of game forms and variations. The paintings show single rope jumping, group single rope jumping, and double-dutch two-rope styles. One painting instructs the rope turners to go "a little slower." Paintings in this cohort document the school's dividing lines, attempts by adults to create play zones for different activities in the school yard, a historic change in the school-yard playscape.

These children captured the surprise of the falling ball. A road appeared alongside winter, although there were no actual roads or snow to be found in the school yard. It was Super Bowl season, and a dozen fifth-graders' images re-created that game, reminding us of the layering of memory and cultural imagery. Smiling, winking, heart-shaped portraits suggest both movement and a growing confidence. And at the same time, the perceived awkwardness of children's bodies comes across in the portrayal of heads as bouncy balls. Both are the same size, having the same roundness, the ball perhaps more expressive than the head. Of the fifth-graders' 41 paintings, only 4 were of icons, 10 showed individual children, and 5 twosomes; groups larger than three were dominant—22, slightly more than half.

The fourth-graders' paintings were filled with more than a dozen portraits: muscular bodies, smiling faces, a Muslim headscarf, and one self-labeled "ugly." There are appeals for help and exclamations such as "SOS" and "Happy Day." "Challenge 1, 2, 3" floats over a jump rope, a traditional chant, a game, and a dare. This game centers on the child in the middle doing fancy moves, the next child repeating her moves and then adding more. Popular among the older children, "Challenge, Challenge" is an improvisation game, like jazz for rope.

Football and basketball are favored in this cohort, but also we see marching and sitting on a bench, supporting the idea that recess is more than a sum of its parts. There are different kinds of activities going on here, and rest may be the most undocumented of all. Out of a total of 56 images, there were 19 individual images, 5 twosomes, 7 with groups of three or more, and 25 cultural icons. These nine-year-olds drew more cultural icons and phrases than any other group: "My besties," or best friends, "Tag-Love," "Broken Song," "Justin Bieber," "Breakfast—Orange Juice, banana," "Love," "Bowl of Soup," "Hello Kitty," "Fish." "This black out. It so Fun and Black."

The third-graders have emotional faces and more portraits with props: "Touchdown Boy," an apologetic "Sorry—Ouch," and another declaration of "Best Friends." There are also statements: "Fall is Fun to Play In" and "Yaa, Wee, You can't get me." Some are ambiguous, like the hybrid commercial admonition "Playless Shop." Among this age set there are only five images of icons, and individual players are more common than either twosomes or larger groups. Perhaps a sign of stretching social groups, one painting shows four children playing in the rain, aligned as two and two in pairs. Another image depicts an invitation to play: three girls offer a fourth a ball.

The most solitary players are in the paintings of the second-graders. More than a dozen images here are of children playing alone, with a half dozen pairs in play, suggesting that one of the functions of recess is to learn to play in groups. One boy painted, "Sprots [Sports] Rule, I love this School"; "I love Recess, I love fun." There are images of jumping rope and basketball, skills that young children are just beginning to practice. Figure 7.12 shows a figure with multiple legs, an illustration style quite common with younger children. Figure 7.13 presents a girl so tall she fills the page. We began with the ten-year-olds as a pictorial reminder that this is the age most likely to lose playtime, yet their images are filled with playing. By ending with the youngest ones, we arrive at the beginning of

Figure 7.10 (Grade 2)

Figure 7.11 (Grade 2)

realism itself, to the portrayal of the child in his or her own emotion-filled body at play.

There were more images of the practice of practice here, rather than the practice of invention per se. This may have something to do with the relatively limited freedom and short amount of time offered for play. As play scholar Brian Sutton-Smith has said, the difference between exploration and play is that exploration asks, "What does it do?" and play asks, "What can I do with it?" Children seem to flip from exploration to play and back again, if given permission and if given time. But unlike a merely scientific process, the goals here are often indirect, with a hidden aesthetic satisfaction, a sincere and layered goofiness.[13]

Figure 7.12 (Grade 2)

Figure 7.13 (Grade 2)

A group of the littlest girls sang when they painted:

Payless SHOES ain't got no GRIP,
Make you FALL and bust your LIP.
FOOT, ain't got no GRIP,
HOP, ain't got no GRIP.
Vanilla PUNCH, vanilla PUNCH,
Make your HEART GO
Two, FORTY, SIX.
ICE cream, ICE cream in a DISH,
HOW many PIECES do you WISH?

Like the paintings, the songs reveal consistencies and novelty. A medley of new and old, sneakers and sweets, the last part is a variation of "Bubble gum, bubble gum in a dish, / How many pieces do you wish?" (because ice cream does not have "pieces," but no matter). When it is sung with a "cherry on top," it echoes an earlier rhyme, "Strawberry shortcake, cream on top, / Tell me the name of your sweetheart." Games, like their players, move.

"My Johnny Lies over the Ocean, My Johnny Lies over the Sea" is this playground's version of "My Bonnie Lies over the Ocean," a Scottish tune going back in print to the 1800s. "Girl Scout, Girl Scout, Do Your Duty" appears in Roger Abrahams's collection of American jump-rope rhymes in the early 1960s. And not only does "Cinderella Dressed in Yella" have a long history, but Cinderella was the star of "the first major Australian publication of children's playlore texts . . . and was banned from the shelves of children's libraries in Australia because of the scatological nature of some of the contents."[14]

According to the Opies' *The Singing Game*, "Miss Mary Mack" combines an old English rhyme and an American one. Traditionally dressed in "black, black, black," in written variations that date back to the 1840s, she now appears in Philadelphia to be dressed in "milk, milk, milk." You can still see children turn a jump rope faster when you hear "red hot pepper"; this tradition goes back to the 1910s in the United Kingdom and has been recorded in the United States since the 1920s.[15] "Miniskirt" and "Nike, Nike" are the newest rhymes recorded here. Our postmodern young woman "knows karate from the front to the back," and she now wears Nikes but won't buy shoes at Payless.[16] Rhymes, then and now, offer

Figure 7.14 (Grade 2)

warnings wrapped in language play; those shoes "ain't got no grip, make you fall and bust your lip."

Like the audio trail of earlier collections, paintlore provides a kind of map of developmental invention. In Philadelphia, tag now has virtual handcuffs. Hoop ball uses hula hoops. I think of Stephan's abstract dashes, the unstuck ball freed with a shoe and a lunchbox. The surreal "Tag-Love, Tag-Love, Tag-Love, Tag-Love." King and Dumbledore. But there is also tremendous consistency here, with great affection remaining for football, jump rope, basketball, and kickball, for professionals in the NBA, for baseball players like the Phillies, football players like the Eagles. The paintings serve as a historical document of what these children play and sing and think about.

Paintings have historically documented culture in the portrayal of everyday games, the most famous image being the painting of children's games by Pieter Bruegel the Elder in 1560. A view of eighty identifiable game forms in a village setting in Belgium, the painting includes blind-

Figure 7.15 (Grade 2)

Figure 7.16 (Grade 2)

man's buff, playing with hoops, wrestling, hide-and-seek, handstands, playing with sand, dolls, leapfrog, and the staging of mock tournaments. The art here is not a psychological portrayal but a valuable historical record of social activity in a particular place and time.

To compare the children's illustrations with the work of the master painter Bruegel might seem absurd. Lev S. Vygotsky argued that the adult imagination is so much more advanced that to suggest children's art is sophisticated goes against the very idea of human development. Contrary to the romantic view of childhood, Vygotsky wrote, "The imagination develops like everything else."[17]

CHAPTER 8

Art Advocacy/Play Advocacy

B ack in 1934, John Dewey wrote in *Art as Experience* that in modern society there is a "chasm between ordinary and esthetic experience."[1] In the name of efficiency we continue to turn many of our schools into assembly lines, eliminating aesthetic, moving, and sensory opportunities in both the classroom and the school yards. Children make no such arbitrary divisions between sensations and information, between motion and thought. For children, the aesthetic is the ordinary way of making sense of the adult world.

In *The Spirit of Folk Art,* Henry Glassie noted that the opposite of aesthetic is *anesthetic*—the deadening of the nerves.[2] Doctors give anesthesia to block the nerves so we will not feel any pain. Ironically, many public schools have become antiseptic, anesthetic places—like hospitals for the disembodied minds of increasingly depressed, obese children. It is as true for children as it is for adults that, as Glassie said, "art is the joy we find in work, surely; it is the record of our bodies bumping through the world, our wits at war with the unknowable."[3]

Postindustrial technology has attempted to bridge the aesthetic chasm with playful tools, placing composing, filming, choreography, and design in the hands of everyone within reach of a computer. But poor children

Figure 8.1 (Grade 2)

Figure 8.2 (Grade 2)

in working-class schools watch from inside the metal fence, without tools and often without art, music, dance, or theater. They do not have much access to technology, let alone simple tools. Before balls were available, poor urban children played with fruit pits, bottle tops, leaves, and rocks.[4] Our urban school yards are sterilized with cement, so there is nothing to invent with, no leaves, no stones, nothing other than the body to experiment with.

As neo-Freudian Donald W. Winnicott wrote in *Playing and Reality,* "The creativity that concerns me here is a universal. It belongs to being alive. . . . [E]verything that happens is creative except in so far as the individual is ill or is hampered by ongoing environmental factors which stifle his creative processes."[5] What is the cost to a generation to find that its environments offer no joy in work, no movement for their bodies, no opportunity for their own wit?

As internationally respected child psychologist David Elkind said, "Today . . . the rich legacy of the grandmasters, supported by an overwhelming amount of contemporary research findings and classroom evidence, is dismissed as irrelevant. . . . The answer, I am afraid, is that what we do in education has little or nothing to do with what we know to be good pedagogy for children."[6]

Figure 8.3 (Grade 2)

The bad news is this:

- It is *normal* for elementary schools to have zero materials to play with at recess.
- It is *normal* for children to have gym once a week as the only time to move their bodies.
- It is *normal* for children to be obese in our culture.
- It is *normal* for us to medicate children so they sit still for seven hours.
- It is *normal* for children to have no art at all.

Today it is *normal* for children to have their whole class of a hundred lose its recess "indefinitely" as a group punishment. Recess Access surveyed all Philadelphia's elementary school yards in 2010 and found that

- 50 percent of school yards were inadequate, meaning that they have broken pavement, poles with no hoops, or teachers' cars parked in the playgrounds.
- 50 percent of the schools studied for this book noted that they have a practice of removing recess as a punishment.
- 30 percent of the schools studied here removed recess at one point during our observation.
- There are still elementary schools in this city that offer no recess at all.

We found that the removal of children's playtime for punishment or "enrichment" is widespread, locally and nationally.[7] This is unfortunately consistent with the picture that researchers are painting about the national decline of recess for children in general and the disappearance of play-related choice time in kindergartens.[8] Recess removal also coincides with budget slashing and its corresponding removal of art, music, and sport programs, a by-product of No Child Left Behind.

Yet, on their turf, these Philadelphia schoolchildren have demonstrated what they can do with two ropes cut from traditional laundry line. They have shown their teachers what three dozen children can do with a newly mounted basketball hoop where none existed before. They have paraded what a tub of tennis balls does for children labeled "special needs"

Figure 8.4 (Grade 2)

and what a bucket of playground balls does for children labeled "trouble." They have shared what three dozen brushes, a bottle of ink, and a case of copy paper brings. Moreover, they have demonstrated that it does not take a lot of money to make a dramatic change in a public school. That's the good news. The best news is that some of the administrators of these nine schools serving 4,500 children are beginning to see these things too.

All nine schools were observed two years after the initial donation. At the two-year mark, six out of nine (two-thirds) were still actively using the supplies, suggesting the long-term value of simple materials. Clearly, donations can make a difference, but there were two schools that continued to punish children by not allowing recess and one that continued to hoard the materials. This implies that for these schools and others like them, there is a need for additional resources and greater advocacy.

New advocates for play and art are emerging in children's museums, departments of parks and recreation, and the medical community. A growing movement of outraged parents now blog about the rise and fall of recess within their towns, and their stories can be found through the website of the American Association for the Child's Right to Play (IPA/USA).[9] In 2013, the United Nations declared its further support for Article 31 of the Convention on the Rights of the Child, its recognition of "the right of the child to rest and leisure, to engage in play and recreational activities . . . and to participate freely in cultural life and the arts."[10]

Among play educators, there is a renewed interest in the open-endedness of loose parts that invite children to carve space and keep time in their own way, to speak in new ways of moving, to practice invention with simple tools. It is ironic that any materials are needed at all to celebrate the aesthetics of the moving child's body on concrete. Is a concrete yard not a stage, ready for performance, ready for design? Yet it is a naked kind of place. Children are drawn to carved, marked spaces, spaces that suggest clues to invention, like the beginnings of a good conversation. The materials give the children permission to create.

This playground of loose parts typically offers children odds and ends, boxes and foam and tires and fabric.[11] One offshoot of the Adventure Playground movement from the United Kingdom, the Play Pod, brings donated materials to schools in a semi-permanent shed that is filled with

Figure 8.5 (Grade 2)

Figure 8.6 (Grade 2)

hoops, foam blocks, fabric, hoses, and other clean industrial material. Both the Play Pods and the Adventure Playground address the needs of flexible, child-designed play, a reaction to the built-by-grown-ups model of climbers fixed in cement. These efforts began when designers noticed that children played with the loose materials left over from the design with greater zeal than the design itself. Like the classic story of the cardboard box being more exciting than the gift, both the Adventure Playgrounds and the Play Pods are built on the idea of recycling cast-off parts, but they cost large amounts of money to run, given the need for additional supervision. Research done by Play Pod and Adventure Playground staff suggests that the additional labor of toy maintenance pays off, given that the necessity of adult interference is far less than the norm. The children are busier, happier, and more focused in their play.[12]

Philadelphia has recently started its own version of the Play Pod with a project called "Free Play on the Parkway," a prop-enhanced temporary outdoor area for parents and their young children. Open-ended materials such as foam and fabric, scoops and sand invite young children to invent in a naturally occurring social space.[13] In New York, architect David Rockwell has created the "Imagination Playground in a Box," which includes large foam blocks and tubes and wheels for open-ended design play for younger and older children. His firm has partnered with playground builder KaBOOM! and the New York City Department of Parks and Recreation. The videos are lovely, invention-filled poems to creativity, but these programs come with a hefty price tag.[14]

The key seems to be not only the novelty of the pieces but the sheer number of objects for children to play with. These pre-packaged playground kits, which require storage, typically include a hundred pieces and weigh more than eight hundred pounds. In addition to entailing a large start-up fee in the several thousands of dollars, the kits again emphasize the need for supervision. But if the materials are light, the children can carry the buckets. If the materials are simple, the costs are manageable for even the most under-resourced community—a few hundred dollars can outfit an entire school.

The challenge to quality play at school is not merely cost. It is a debate over the culture of schooling and of our societal investment in creative practice. If we accept that children have their own folk arts and their own peer culture, a mix of play and art—singing, dancing, drawing, acting, sport—then we can envision the enrichment of children's cultural vitality.

What is cultural vitality? The Urban Institute's Arts and Culture Indicators Project in Washington, D.C., defines cultural vitality as "evidence of creating, disseminating, validating, and supporting arts and culture as a dimension of everyday life."[15] Vitality is made up of status, demography, and institutional support. Status can be economic status, social status, sociohistorical status, or language status. Demography reflects distribution, territory, concentration, proportion, and sheer numbers of participants. Institutional support consists of both formal and informal support.[16]

Figure 8.7 (Grade 2)

Figure 8.8 (Grade 2)

Cultural vitality can be related to what sociolinguists such as Miriam Meyerhoff call "ethnolinguistic vitality." Ethnolinguistic vitality is "a measure of the strength and liveliness of a language, usually a good indicator of the likelihood that it will gradually die out or continue to be used as the living language of a community. . . . A linguistic variety has relatively high 'vitality' if it is spoken and used widely."[17]

If we accept that play and art are like languages, we can speak of children's cultural vitality, its demographics, and its institutional support. If it is normal in a place not to support children's play at recess or children's art opportunities, then we can say that this place does not have a vital children's culture (unless we are examining only underground or illicit forms). If children have supported access to art and play, we can begin to document their growth and fluency. We know that when children are denied opportunities to express themselves, to digest their own thoughts, or to

Figure 8.9 (Grade 2)

practice the realignment of their social worlds, they become depressed, agitated, or even violent.

Studies of ethnolinguistic vitality carry out a census-like tally of native speakers to monitor a language's vibrancy and its active use. The same can be done for people, organizations, and forms of documentation that speak "play" *and* "art." Do children in a particular context have materials? Do they play anyway? Do they have consistent formal and informal support for their activities? Do they have consistent everyday time to express themselves? Beyond the basic institutional questions of classroom instruction, what kind of movement languages, visual grammars, and sound vocabularies are there? What traditions are being honored or suppressed? Which children are being denied play, and are there patterns by age, gender, race, ethnicity, or class? How do the official policies compare with what actually occurs in everyday life?

These are socio-cultural questions, not merely psychological ones. Our society is used to a psychological discussion about children's mental health, or a medical discussion about physical ailments like obesity. We have separate academic subjects dealing with different aspects of the child's body, separate advocacy groups fighting over funds, each addressing different aspects of the city's ailments. The wisdom of the playground is that resilience, health, and creative thinking are more layered, more social, and more fluid than we adults have assumed in our isolated static institutions.

Philadelphia is a financially broken city with rich resources of the imagination. If we let them, artists and movement specialists can help revitalize our school agendas, just as murals have helped us reimagine the boundaries of our neighborhoods. But if we stop there, the paint peels, the weeds grow, and despair returns. Instead of succumbing to the helplessness of postindustrial poverty, it makes sense return to the aesthetic experiences of other, leaner times. If we want children's culture to be vibrant, we have to find ways to encourage each child to bounce symbols, tickle power, and kick around ideas.

Recess Access has distributed thousands of brochures created especially for children who have lost their recess in order to encourage parental advocacy. They were freely distributed in recreation centers, bicycle shops, pediatricians' offices, bakeries, supermarkets, libraries, dentists' offices, toy stores, and elementary schools. Speaking engagements and interviews

Figure 8.10 (Grade 2)

in print, on the web, and over radio have been met with enthusiasm, and new partnerships are emerging between organizations serving children. By the time this book is published, even more schools will have been out-fitted with materials. With every donation of jump ropes, balls, hoops, and chalk comes a reminder of the health value of play, how play serves children physically, emotionally, socially, and culturally. It is ironic that children's physical, emotional, social, and cultural vitality may depend on a ball, a rope, and a stick of chalk.

Megan LaMon

Conclusion

The Practice of Invention

So what, then, is the relationship between artistry and children's art, between art itself and play? Do artists simply create from within, from a place of individual genius, and do children play with what romantically emerges from inside their own heads? The playground and the artists suggest that some kind of stimulation is necessary, that we do not just play; we play off of something. We do not just create; we react; we move and remove.

Peter Rose, filmmaker:

> For me, there are two modes of creative enterprise, one arising from intention and the other from play. Early on I realized that film was a form of mathematics, that you could build things in space and time by playing with the individual frames of the medium. So my work at that point often started from a premise, a concept, an algorithm, a structure whose unfolding interested me. . . . But there is a whole other way of working, which is much more purely intuitive, more genuinely playful.

For example, I have a flip camera, which I love to use to shoot on my various desultory outings. I had about three years' worth of footage in my files that I hadn't really looked at. So recently, I went through all this stuff and tagged the images I found interesting, looking for some grammar of my own curiosity. I gathered a bunch of these together and then I started playing with them, seeing if there were images that had anything to do with one another, if there were hidden themes to my random acts of attention.

So I started grouping these together, and there'd be little accidents of juxtaposition in the editing that led me into unforeseen directions. . . . Slowly, if you are lucky, some kind of poetic utterance emerges from all this playing around and you take full credit for it as an intentional act, full well knowing that this is a bit misleading.

Working with digital cameras, there are accidents that happen, like shooting them from the wrong place. Then I'll go along—say I've superimposed it for some accidental reason. Hmm. Why is this working? It is a chance factor. Then I'll ask, "Why is it interesting?" and apply that principle to other material. We're talking about discovery, and capitalizing on it.

I work against the industrial model—scripted, rational, planning required. I'm pushing something intuitive, spontaneous, and risky. I tell you when you get out of school you have to justify everything. This is the time in your life when you can play. To head them off in this direction, I give them a rather difficult assignment that involves catching a decisive moment—a particular event, a meaningful composition that arises all by itself, some peculiarity of nature that's worth looking at. It's about being in the right place at the right time and being receptive. It's a kind of playful looking.

Another issue, how we get into play. That's quite tricky. You can't sit down and make something deliberately. So I go into my studio and neaten things up like housekeeping. I tidy up the equipment, then I tidy up my pens, and then you end up organizing the images and the sounds and playing with them a bit. I go into it sideways, through organizational housecleaning. Half the time I go into my studio to neaten things up, I come out four hours later.

After the discoveries, you have to have discipline to find what's interesting and see if what you've made is clear enough. The joy comes in those moments of discovery. The craft is evaluating the quality of the sound, finessing the image. Sometimes this process can take quite a long time.

I had a poem I wanted to narrate, an original poem about seeing into space. It was banal just to hear it. You needed to read it, as it was better mediated through reading. At that point, subtitles were only used in foreign films. I thought, what should that language be? So I invented a language, with the same rhythm, so you would have an excuse to read the subtitles. I went for rhythm and general parallelism, very romance-language-based. Later on, I got permission to climb the Golden Gate Bridge. I discovered that if you put those shots together, you became habituated to it and the film lost its drama. To give you a reprieve from the images, I inserted black frames, and black became an intermittent experience. This took seven years.

Then I wanted to do a cheap, fast, loose, slightly zany version. Why don't I take the invented language and create a second film, with all black? Just the words. Two incipient ideas ended up fusing into a whole new piece. The unresolved in one piece merged into another; it played into another.

. . .

I asked Manfred Fischbeck, choreographer, musician, about art and play:

Play? It's at the core.

All of the focus in music, or dance, comes out of game or play. And I think that it helps so much, if you think of play or games as one of focus. Play, moving from your shoulder, you play with the self. You take off judging, self-consciousness. You get involved with playing with your own body. There is a magical thing that happens—you forget about thinking. You stop thinking and you start playing. And this works on all different levels. It works with kids, and sixty-year-olds, and it works with dance students.

The biggest enemy in the dance studio is the mirror. They try to make it look like something. Then it's dead, already gone. They didn't feel it. They judge it, have a preconceived image, and then it's lifeless. They don't have experience making something or creating. We have to get them out of their prisons, of "this one way is right and that's wrong" prison.

Figure C.1 (Grade 2)

The preparation always for playing or improvising is that you need to have a moment of meditation, but I am not calling it that. Setting up a moment of being still and introducing a way of engaging with the body. I can't say, "Now, start dancing." But, "Shift your weight, side to side . . ."

Last week I did this structure with verbalized movement. It started by verbalizing, "I lift my hand out.". . . I then pushed them—talk about the feeling of it, the image of it. All of a sudden it became poetry, without thinking about it. Out of a playfulness, out of having fun. It was clear when that added dimension moved from analytical to associative for people who say, "I can't improvise, I can't choreograph." Some dancers, when I say, "Do something with words," they die, and so the play aspect of it breaks the barrier.

Anna Beresin:

Where do your games come from?

Manfred Fischbeck:

The impetus to develop this form was when we were in Berlin and saw the Living Theater in 1964 or '65, one performance called "Mysteries." One of them was a game with two lines of people. One person steps into the center and creates a movement character and ends up with a certain pattern that is transferred to the groups on the side. Then this pattern is picked up by everyone, and then the person exchanges places and the next person does it, very ritualistic. This was an eye-opener for us, as a structure, a movement game. Then we began to practice that in the studio with a chamber group we had in Berlin.

I was just beginning to dance in Philadelphia some years later. I was doing my first performance here in Philadelphia. Because we worked with people who weren't dancers (it had something to do with teaching visual artists here at the Philadelphia College of Art, now The University of the Arts), we started to work, bring these people into the company. We needed to find forms, movement forms, that they could do without having "technique." For instance, using a form like crystallization and then being able to perform.

So games started to emerge as a way of deriving movement forms, one after the other after the other. Starting in 1971, we honed in on that.

Anna Beresin:

Do kids do the same thing as artists?

Manfred Fischbeck:

I think they are the same. I really do, in the initial moment.

In the evolution of things, it's where the skill comes into play. When we do the workshops, people who come for the first time almost always say, "I felt like a kid," with a memory of that creative being that kids have. The wonder of just imagining, becoming something. The way I see it, both sides of the brain are not so separate for children, so they are constantly feeding each other in the same way that artists re-create.

From my own experience with my own children, when they were drawing, painting—nobody had to tell them. When they go to school, they hear, "What is this? This is not a tree. *This* is what a tree is." Right and wrong are imposed; creativity was pushed under. Creativity was diminished. The ritual impulse of play that leads to expression, imagery; that has to be the initial impulse to make art. I can't see it any other way. Then skill kicks in.

When I play music improvisationally for dance, I find when I am just watching, when I start thinking in skill forms in terms of scale, tempo, key, it flattens, it becomes constricted and has no life. It is this engagement, the interplay that my skill will support, and do without thinking.

I want to make my dancers understand, creating is like dreaming. Why do we dream at night? We create paintings, movies. Why are we doing this? I always tell my students the story of sleep deprivation. Dreaming is not just a luxury. A lot of the most creative kids end up in psychiatric care, because they're not allowed to follow their dreaming.

You can make art without play, I just wouldn't expect it to be very good.

Figure C.2 (Grade 2)

Ritualized, exaggerated, juxtapositions are the terms here. From playful looking to playful moving, these moments tend to happen in stimulating, transitional times and spaces, in the in-between, the inter-*lude*, the straightening up, the before-the-dance, the recess. The artists then trust the legitimacy of their thinking, the validity of their right to move ideas as part of their creative practice.

In *Art, Mind, Brain,* Howard Gardner referred to philosopher Nelson Goodman's idea that there are two distinguishing elements between children's art and artists' art: both have an expressive, emotional element, but the artist, the skilled practiced one, has a sense of mastery or repleteness, and chooses among an assortment of techniques to express the artistic idea. Gardner also asserted that this expressive skill, so readily found in the art of young children, disappears during the school-age years, suggesting a poverty of expression in children's concrete thinking.[1]

These children's paintings and the playground games show two other areas emerging in the world of the school-age child that reveal sophistication rather than a poverty of skill. One is a sense of wit, of clever composition, that often emerges as artist Phillip Schulman's "happy accident." The other skill, closely related to this, is the idea of social awareness, or of interpersonal intelligence, as Gardner described it in his work on multiple intelligences.[2] Children's art in chalk, ink, and play reflects a social interrelatedness, a layering of cultural truths, no matter the degree of technical skill.

The artists, regardless of discipline, all described a need for play as a way to refresh their thinking, to keep things "open" within their disciplined form. Actor David Howey prepares his students for Shakespeare with playground games. Choreographer Brian Sanders utilizes real playgrounds as a studio for novel movement. Fine artist Carol Moore says that creating involves "physically moving things around." Discipline comes later. Composer Evan Solot says, "There is that feeling of delight when an idea works—either because that spot has a potential solution and/or that it's leading me into new possibilities." Musician Ron Kerber notes, "You want to be surprised. You want to be tickled."

As Charles Darwin reminds us, it is just not possible to tickle yourself.[3] We need others, or stand-ins for others—like novel materials—to tickle us. Jonas Milder, industrial designer, talked with me about the practice of design and his wish for a return to play: "I would make things bigger, smaller, then put them on top of each other, back to building blocks. Play and design is such that you keep it open. The process collapses on itself if

Figure C.3 (Grade 2)

you don't keep it open. I look for parts that grabbed my interest. How can I use that? You try it. Does it work? Doesn't it work? I am looking for ways to bring that back."

Psychologist Jerome Bruner wrote of this as "effective surprise": "I would propose that all of the forms of effective surprise grow out of combinatorial activity—a placing of things in new perspectives." And: "What is characteristic of the great work of art is that its metaphoric artifice, its juxtapositions, have not only surprise value but illuminating honesty."[4]

Expressive skill is still the realm of the young child. Technical mastery is clearly the realm of the artist, as he or she yearns for the younger child's expressive skill. What the school-age child brings to the drawing table is this sense of accidental wit, along with an increasing social intelligence. As the children rehearse being more competitive, more solitary, more cooperative, more sneaky, more tender, more direct, and more indirect, they use props that bounce, swing, and drop in unpredictable ways. Then they do all this in relation to the other players: "Spit, spit, you are not it." "Challenge, challenge, 1, 2, 3." Invention is then tickled through the exaggerated play of games.

The artists here circle back to play, the players to practicing their proto-arts, the young painters to capturing the vitality of their moves. Hardly trivial, the playground and the studio remind us of the physicality of hope:

> for Darnell, who cuts his way into a paper limo,
> for Claire, who parodies Lil Wayne,
> for the one who liberates her classmates from handcuffs, and
> for the boys who pretend to be Eagles.

Megan LaMon

Acknowledgments

T he book would not exist without the encouragement, good cheer, and hard work of many people. My gratitude goes to Rama Chorpash, director of product design at Parsons The New School for Design, and Wendy Smith in Organizational Behavior at the Lerner School of Business at the University of Delaware, both of whom served as advisers in the framing of Recess Access. We met weekly for several months, sharing resources and brainstorming about the most effective ways to help urban children. Wendy helped solicit donors as she spoke about her field of paradox theory—the idea, much like play, that organizations can say yes to a variety of seemingly conflicting needs. Rama helped with our first brochure: "A Simple Solution Beckons." Our interplay led to the most fun project in my academic career so far.

My thanks to colleagues and UARTS administrators Donna Faye Burchfield, Chris Garvin, Neil Kleinman, Catherine Kodat, Will McHale, Connie Michael, Chris Myers, Peter Stambler, Beth van Why, and Provost Kirk Pillow for their encouragement. The project began with funding from The University of the Arts as a start-up initiative of the Philadelphia Applied Research Laboratory and was sustained by additional funding from the Provost's Office. Additional funds came from total strangers after an interview about my book *Recess Battles* appeared in the *Philadelphia Inquirer*, thanks to writer Art Carey. WHYY's Marty Moss-Coane was kind to promote *The Art of Play* on National Public Radio even before it was published.

Ten professors, all at The University of the Arts, were particularly good sports in agreeing to be interviewed for this book. It is my honor to work with such master players: Manfred Fischbeck, Nancy Heller, David Howey, Ron Kerber, Jonas Milder, Carol Moore, Peter Rose, Brian Sanders, Phillip Schulman, and Evan Solot. Students from my Game Play class in Multimedia were instrumental in surveying the city's school yards. Volunteers from my Observing Children class were extremely helpful in hauling supplies to Philadelphia schools. The initial crew of Recess Access cut rope, labeled buckets, sorted donations, and tested pedometers. To you I will always be grateful: Lauren DeAngelis, Megan LaMon, Naima Mirella, Brie Stevens, Leslie Zacharkow, and team captain Christine Zapata. Keep playing.

I appreciate the advice and permission from the School District of Philadelphia for various projects described in the book, especially from Ms. Bettyann Creighton, Mrs. Abigail Jiménez-Padrón, Mr. Daniel Sapon, and the dozens of principals, gym teachers, and art teachers I promised not to name. Thanks to Daniel T. Cook, professor of childhood studies at Rutgers University, Camden; Richard M. Heiberger, professor of statistics at Temple University; Maddy Cantor, professor of dance at Bryn Mawr College; Kathy Schultz, dean of education at Mills College; activist Susan Landau; and Roni Anton of the Project Learn School.

A thumbs-up to Mira Adornetto and JohnPaul Beattie of The University of the Arts Faculty Tech Center for making me look good. Taylor and Francis, publisher of the new *International Journal of Play*, graciously allowed me to reprint excerpts from "Play Counts: Pedometers and the Case for Recess" (1, no.2 [September 2012]: 131–138), and Mick Gusinde-Duffy, senior acquisitions editor at Temple University Press, did not even flinch when I proposed this book to him. The encouragement of executive editor Micah Kleit and copyeditor Kim Vivier meant a great deal. If I wore a hat, I would tip it to Kate Nichols and her art team for the careful reproduction of the children's drawings. Many thanks.

A high five to arts activist and long-time friend Amy Chin for introducing me to the Village of the Arts and Humanities, to Lily Yeh for founding it, and to art teachers Joan Fox and Debby Pollack for taking me there. The Village has served as a point of inspiration for our Recess Access volunteers, and we thank the staff and the members of the community for making us feel welcome. To Marge and Sy Richman, Connie and Carl Beresin, and all my friends and family who donated materials to Recess Access—thank you. My proceeds from *The Art of Play* will be donated back to Recess Access; with these small funds we can do a lot of good for a great number of children. To learn more about recess donations and children's play advocacy, visit www.recessaccess.org.

A shout-out to those young artists whose work appears in this book, who spoke with ink on their brushes and ink on their faces. To the hundreds of direct participants in Recess Access, and the thousands of potential players—I am in awe of what you can do with a concrete slab when given twenty minutes and some simple materials. Most of all, thanks to Neil, Noah, Matti, and Gabe, for reminding me why this matters.

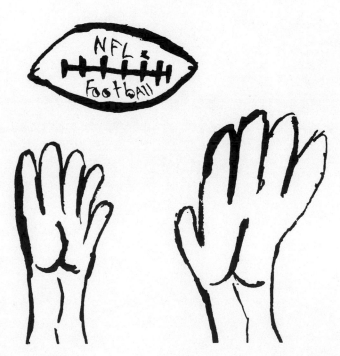

Figure A.1 (Grade 5)

Notes

INTRODUCTION

1. See www.greatschools.org.

2. Sutton-Smith 1972, 1981.

3. Bronner 1988. For a fine examination of the anthropology of African folk toys, see Rossie 2005.

4. Kirshenblatt and Kirshenblatt-Gimblett 2007, 381–382.

5. For further discussion of the paradoxical essence of play, see Bateson 1972 and Sutton-Smith 1997. For an explanation of playground paradoxes, see Beresin 2010.

6. Fantuzzo et al. 2005; Fantuzzo and Sutton-Smith et al. 1996; Paley 2010, 1988; Reynolds and Jones 1997.

7. Fineberg 1997, 2006; Gardner 1982; Root-Bernstein and Root-Bernstein 1999.

8. Sutton-Smith 1997, 133–135.

9. Gardner 1980, 269.

10. Fineberg 2006 has a particularly fine annotated chronology of scholarship about children's art and the history of children's art on display.

11. Sutton-Smith 1997; Heller 2002.

12. For further discussion of modern art as being misunderstood and called childlike, see Heller 2002, 68–69. Gardner (1982) noted, "As Picasso once remarked, 'I used to draw like Raphael, but it has taken me a whole lifetime to

learn to draw like a child'" (89). The child was the romanticized, free "other" who inspired constrained modern artists to see beyond their training. See Fineberg 1997.

13. Sully 1895, 321–322.

14. Johnson 1987.

15. Freud 1907, 143–149.

16. Gardner 1982, 102.

17. Jemie 2003.

18. Factor 2009; Marsh 2008.

CHAPTER 3. CHALK

1. Caillois 1961, 64.

2. Huizinga 1955, 129.

3. For further discussion of the dilemmas of adult intervention, see Sutton-Smith and Sutton-Smith 1974. For a detailed account of preschool children as master players, see Fantuzzo et al. 1996 and 2005, Paley 1988, and Reynolds and Jones 1997.

4. Escobedo (1999, 101–122) described how drawing for young children is a performance art, much as it is for our singing painters: "Drawing may serve as a dramatic medium" (103); "Children engage in various play activities while drawing" (120); "Jeremy joins Kiah and Leila in the social drama while Walter comments on the action. There was much movement and loud verbalization" (118).

5. One could say that any grown-up who hands out donated chalk in the School District is also a troublemaker. Appealing to nostalgia helps to avoid hassles.

6. For more information or to plan a visit, see www.villagearts.org.

CHAPTER 6. "WE INVENTED IT"/"WE TAUGHT THEM"

1. The study was submitted to the Institutional Review Board and was approved by the board and by the Office of Research and Evaluation at the School District of Philadelphia.

2. Each "Multiple-Function Pedometer by Robic" was set to zero and attached horizontally to a child-sized, Velcro belt, which the children placed on their waists and which were inspected by researchers.

3. Using a blocked one-way analysis of variance, with "Locations" as the treatment and "Children" as the blocks, the ANOVA data show that the treatment difference between average gym count and average recess count is significant at $p = 10–5$, or $p = 0.00001$.

4. Using the term "descriptive epidemiology," one recent pedometer study "demonstrated the viability of using relatively inexpensive pedometers and methods" in the study of young people's activities (Craig et al. 2010). A previous study of American children's pedometer use (Brusseau 2008) also found that, per minute, free play offers more movement than gym. The rates were similar to our study for both gym and recess. Unlike Brusseau's findings, and the findings of Beighle et al. (2006) and Cardon et al. (2008), we found girls and boys to be equally active. In an earlier study among Australian children by Lindsay and Palmer (1981), playtime was also associated with more vigorous activity than physical education classes.

5. Beresin 2010.

6. Factor 2009, 1.

7. Laban and Lawrence 1947; Guest 2005; McCaw 2011.

8. Laban 1960, 17.

9. Salen and Zimmerman 2004, 304.

10. Erikson 1950.

11. Piaget 1932.

12. Vygotsky 1978; Winnicott 1971.

13. Sutton-Smith, 1997.

14. Sutton-Smith 1997.

15. Taylor 2011. See the American Academy of Pediatrics policy statement, "The Crucial Role of Recess in School" (Murray and Ramstetter 2013).

CHAPTER 7. THE PAINTLORE OF CHILDREN

1. In her fine book *The Pictorial World of the Child* (2005), Maureen Cox has a chapter titled "Cultural Influence on Children's Artwork." Especially interesting are images of a classroom in Tanzania done by a ten-year-old, with a big teacher in the center and tiny three-to-a-person desks. These are contrasted with a ten-year-old Swede's image of one child equal in size to the teacher, who is off to the side.

2. For a critique of stage theories of artistic development, see Kindler and Darras 1997. For a classic on children and art, see Lewis 1966.

3. Art educator Viktor Lowenfeld said, "Children who are silent and have no desire to express themselves are not healthy children" (Brittain 1968, 57). The same can be said of children who do not play.

4. For a fine example of play therapy and multimodal art therapy, see Axline 1947.

5. Coles 1986b, 149.

6. Coles 1986b, 206.

7. Coles 1990, 40.

8. Mitchell 2006, 60.

9. For more on the comparative study of younger children's drawings across culture, see Alland 1983.

10. For more on the verb as a theme in the storytelling of young children, see Sutton-Smith 1981. For a collection of games framed in verbs, see Opie and Opie 1969.

11. See Piaget 1932; Piaget and Inhelder 1948.

12. See Dewey 1934.

13. For more about the art of practicing, see Kurtz 2007. One of the finest books on improvisation is Johnstone 1979.

14. Marsh 2008, 48.

15. Abrahams 1969, 115. For examples of spice related to speed in other cultures, see Butler 1989, 146.

16. Newell (1998) wrote of the "inventiveness of children" and the "conservatism of children," meaning that even as children hold on to the sacredness of what their peers and elder siblings and cousins have shown them, they also adapt and invent new forms of culture. They invent, and they also practice.

17. Vygotsky 2004, 32.

CHAPTER 8. ART ADVOCACY/PLAY ADVOCACY

1. Dewey 1934, 10.

2. Glassie 1989, 63.

3. Glassie 1989, 258.

4. See Dargan and Zeitlin's fine photographic essay (1990) and Opie and Opie 1997.

5. Winnicott 1971, 67–68.

6. Quoted in Miller and Almon 2009, 3.

7. Barros et al. 2009; Beresin 2010; Patte 2009.

8. Robert Wood Johnson Foundation 2010; Miller and Almon 2009; Patte 2009; Stokes-Guinan 2009.

9. www.ipausa.org.

10. www2.ohchr.org/english/bodies/crc/docs/GC/CRC-C-GC-17_en.doc.

11. See Nicholson 1972 for an introduction to the idea of loose parts.

12. See www.playpod.co.uk; Allen 1950, 1968.

13. See www.playinbetween.com.

14. Visit www.imaginationplayground.com or www.kaboom.org.

15. Jackson et al. 2006, 4.

16. Jackson et al. 2006, 12.

17. Meyerhoff 2006, 108.

CONCLUSION: THE PRACTICE OF INVENTION

1. Gardner (1980, 8) quoted critic Andre Malraux: "Though a child is often artistic, he is not an artist. For his gift controls him; not he his gift." He further noted that Maria Montessori agreed, as did painter Paul Klee.

2. Gardner 1983.

3. See Darwin (1872) 2009.

4. Bruner 1962, 20 and 14.

References

Abrahams, Roger. 1969. *Jump-rope rhymes: A dictionary.* Publications of the American Folklore Society. Vol. 20. Austin: University of Texas Press.

Alland, Alexander, Jr. 1983. *Playing with form: Children draw in six cultures.* New York: Columbia University Press.

Allen of Hurtwood, Lady (Marjory Gill Allen). 1950. *Adventure playgrounds.* London: National Playing Fields Association.

———. 1968. *Planning for play.* Cambridge, MA: MIT Press.

Axline, Virginia. 1947. *Play therapy: The inner dynamics of childhood.* Boston: Houghton Mifflin.

Barros, Romina M., Ellen J. Silver, and Ruth E. K. Stein. 2009. "School recess and group classroom behavior." *Pediatrics* 123, no. 2 (February): 431–436.

Bateson, Gregory. 1972. *Steps to an ecology of mind.* New York: Ballantine.

Beighle, A., C. F. Morgan, G. Le Masurier, and R. P. Pangrazi. 2006. "Children's physical activity during recess and outside of school." *Journal of School Health* 76, no. 10 (December): 516–520.

Beresin, Anna R. 2010. *Recess battles: Playing, fighting, and storytelling.* Jackson: University Press of Mississippi.

Brittain, W. Lambert. 1968. *Viktor Lowenfeld speaks on art and creativity.* Reston, VA: National Art Education Association.

Bronner, Simon. 1988. *American children's folklore.* Little Rock, AR: August House.

Bruner, Jerome. 1962. *On knowing: Essays for the left hand.* Cambridge, MA: Belknap Press of Harvard University Press.

Brusseau, T. A. 2008. "Pedometer-determined physical activity patterns of fourth and fifth grade children." PhD diss., Arizona State University. University Microfilms no. 3303243.

Butler, Francelia. 1989. *Skipping around the world: The ritual nature of folk rhymes.* Hamden, CT: Library Professional Publications.

Caillois, Roger. 1961. *Man, play, and games.* New York: Free Press of Glencoe.

Cardon, G., E. Van Cauwenberghe, V. Labarque, L. Haerens, and L. De Bourdeaudhuij. 2008. "The contribution of preschool playground factors in explaining children's physical activity during recess." *International Journal of Behavior Nutrition and Physical Activity* 5 (February 26): 11.

Coles, Robert. 1986a. *The moral life of children.* Boston: Atlantic Monthly Press.

———. 1986b. *The political life of children.* Boston: Atlantic Monthly Press.

———. 1990. *The spiritual life of children.* Boston: Houghton Mifflin.

———. 1992. *Their eyes meeting the world: The drawings and paintings of children.* Edited by Margaret Sartor. Boston: Houghton Mifflin.

Cox, Maureen. 2005. *The pictorial world of the child.* Cambridge: Cambridge University Press.

Craig, C., C. Cameron, J. Griffiths, and C. Tudor-Locke. 2010. "Descriptive epidemiology of youth pedometer-determined physical activity: CANPLAY." *Medicine and Science in Sports and Exercise* 42, no. 9 (September): 1639–1643.

Dargan, Amanda, and Steven Zeitlin. 1990. *City play.* New Brunswick, NJ: Rutgers University Press.

Darwin, Charles. 2009. *The expression of the emotions in man and animals.* 3rd ed. Oxford: Oxford University Press. First published in 1872.

Dewey, John. 1934. *Art as experience.* New York: Minton, Balch and Co.

Erikson, Erik. 1950. *Childhood and society.* New York: Norton.

Escobedo, Theresa H. 1999. "The canvas of play: A study of children's play behaviors while drawing." In *Play and culture studies, volume 2: Play contexts revisited,* edited by Stuart Reifel, 101–122. Stamford, CT: Ablex.

Factor, June. 2009. "It's only play if you get to choose." *Play and Culture Studies* 9 (1): 129–146.

Fantuzzo, John, Patricia Manz, Marc Atkins, and Raymond Meyers. 2005. "Peer-mediated treatment of socially withdrawn maltreated preschool children: Cultivating natural community resources." *Journal of Clinical Child and Adolescent Psychology* 34 (2): 322–327.

Fantuzzo, John, and Brian Sutton-Smith et al. 1996. "Community-based resilient peer treatment of withdrawn maltreated preschool children." *Journal of Consulting and Clinical Psychology* 64 (6): 1377–1386.

Fineberg, Jonathan. 1997. *The innocent eye: Children's art and the modern artist.* Princeton, NJ: Princeton University Press.

———. 2006. *When we were young: New perspectives on the art of the child.* Berkeley: University of California Press.

Freud, Sigmund. 1907. "Creative writers and day-dreaming." In *The standard edition of the complete psychological works of Sigmund Freud, vol. 9 (1906–1908),* edited by James Strachey et al. London: Hogarth Press. Reprinted in *On Freud's "Creative writers and day-dreaming,"* edited by E. S. Person et al., 143–149. New Haven, CT: Yale University Press, 1995.

Gardner, Howard. 1980. *Artful scribbles: The significance of children's drawings.* New York: Basic Books.

————. 1982. *Art, mind, and brain: A cognitive approach to creativity.* New York: Basic Books.

————. 1983. *Frames of mind: The theory of multiple intelligences.* New York: Basic Books.

Glassie, Henry. 1989. *The spirit of folk art: The Girard Collection at the Museum of International Folk Art.* New York: Harry N. Abrams.

Gomme, Lady Alice B. 1894. *Traditional games of England, Scotland, and Ireland, with tunes, singing-rhymes, and methods of playing according to the variants extant and recorded in different parts of the kingdom.* London: D. Nutt.

Guest, Ann H. 2005. *Labanotation: The system for analyzing and recording movement.* New York: Routledge.

Heller, Nancy. 2002. *Why a painting is like a pizza.* Princeton, NJ: Princeton University Press.

Huizinga, Johan. 1955. *Homo ludens: A study of the play-element in culture.* Boston: Beacon Press.

Jackson, Maria Rosario, Florence Kabwasa-Green, and Joaquín Herranz. 2006. *Cultural vitality in communities: Interpretation and indicators.* Available at http://www.urban.org/UploadedPDF/311392_Cultural_Vitality.pdf. Washington, DC: Urban Institute.

Jemie, Onwuchekwa. 2003. *Yo' mama! New raps, toasts, dozens, jokes, and children's rhymes from urban Black America.* Philadelphia: Temple University Press.

Johnson, Mark. 1987. *The body in the mind: The bodily basis of meaning, imagination, and reason.* Chicago: University of Chicago Press.

Johnstone, Keith. 1979. *Impro: Improvisation and the theatre.* New York: Theatre Arts.

Kindler, Anna M., and Bernard Darras. 1997. "Map of artistic development." In *Child development in art,* edited by Anna M. Kindler, 17–43. Reston, VA: National Art Education Association.

Kirshenblatt, Mayer, and Barbara Kirshenblatt-Gimblett. 2007. *They called me Mayer July: Painted memories of a Jewish childhood in Poland before the Holocaust.* Berkeley: University of California Press.

Kurtz, Glenn. 2007. *Practicing: A musician's return to music.* New York: Vintage Books.

Laban, Rudolf. 1960. *The mastery of movement.* London: Macdonald and Evans.

Laban, Rudolf, and F. C. Lawrence. 1947. *Effort.* Boston: Macdonald and Evans.

Lewis, Hilda Present. 1966. *Child art: Beginnings of self-affirmation.* Berkeley: Diablo Press.

Lindsay, P. L., and D. Palmer. 1981. *Playground game characteristics of Brisbane primary school children.* ERDC Report no. 28. Canberra: Australian Government Publishing Service.

Marsh, Kathryn. 2008. *The musical playground: Global tradition and change in children's songs and games.* Oxford: Oxford University Press.

McCaw, Dick. 2011. "Laban's concept of effort and his work in the 1940s and 1950s." In *The Laban sourcebook,* edited by Dick McCaw, 197–206. London: Routledge.

Meyerhoff, Miriam. 2006. *Introducing sociolinguistics.* New York: Routledge.

Miller, Edward, and Joan Almon. 2009. *Crisis in kindergarten: Why children need to play in school.* College Park, MD: Alliance for Childhood.

Mitchell, Lisa M. 2006. "Child-centered? Thinking critically about children's drawings as visual research method." *Visual Anthropology Review* 22 (1): 60–73.

Murray, Robert, and Catherine Ramstetter. 2013. "The crucial role of recess in school." Council on School Health. *Pediatrics* 131 (1): 183–188, doi:10.1542/peds.2012-2993.

Newell, William Wells. 1998. *The games and songs of American children*. Baltimore, MD: Clearfield. Originally published in 1884.

Nicholson, Simon. 1972. "The theory of loose parts: An important principle for design methodology." *Studies in Design Education, Craft and Technology* 4, no. 2, http://ojs.lboro.ac.uk/ojs/index.php/SDEC/article/view/1204.

Opie, Iona, and Peter Opie. 1969. *Children's games in street and playground*. Oxford: Oxford University Press.

———. 1985. *The singing game*. Oxford: Oxford University Press.

———. 1997. *Children's games with things*. Oxford: Oxford University Press.

Paley, Vivian Gussen. 1988. *Bad guys don't have birthdays: Fantasy play at four*. Chicago: University of Chicago Press.

———. 2010. *Boy on the beach: Building community through play*. Chicago: University of Chicago Press.

Patte, Michael. 2009. "The state of recess in Pennsylvania elementary schools: A continuing tradition or distant memory?" *Play and Culture Studies* 9 (1): 147–165.

Piaget, Jean. 1932. *The moral judgment of the child*. Reprint, New York: Free Press, 1965.

Piaget, Jean, and Barbel Inhelder. 1948. *The child's conception of space*. Reprint, London: Routledge, 1967.

Reynolds, Gretchen, and Elizabeth Jones. 1997. *Master players: Learning from children at play*. New York: Teachers College Press.

Robert Wood Johnson Foundation. 2010. *The state of play: Gallup survey of principals on school recess*. Princeton, NJ: Robert Wood Johnson Foundation.

Root-Bernstein, Robert S., and Michele Root-Bernstein. 1999. *Sparks of genius: The thirteen thinking tools of the world's most creative people*. New York: Houghton Mifflin.

Rossie, Jean-Pierre. 2005. *Toys, play, culture and society: An anthropological approach with reference to North Africa and the Sahara*. Stockholm: SITREC.

Salen, Katie, and Eric Zimmerman. 2004. *Rules of play: Game design fundamentals*. Cambridge, MA: MIT Press.

Stokes-Guinan, Katie. 2009. "Child's play: Why increasing opportunities to play and be active may improve students' academic and physical outcomes." Literature review. John W. Gardner Center for Youth and Their Communities, Stanford University.

Sully, James. 1895. *Studies of childhood*. London: Longmans Green.

Sutton-Smith, Brian. 1972. *The folkgames of children*. Publications of the American Folklore Society. Vol. 24. Austin: University of Texas Press.

———. 1981. *The folkstories of children*. Publications of the American Folklore Society. New series. Vol. 3. Philadelphia: University of Pennsylvania Press.

———. 1997. *The ambiguity of play*. Cambridge, MA: Harvard University Press.

Sutton-Smith, Brian, and Shirley Sutton-Smith. 1974. *How to play with your children (and when not to)*. New York: Hawthorn Books.

Taylor, Daniel. 2011. "A Philadelphia pediatrician writes of the sickening effects of childhood obesity." *Philadelphia Inquirer*, August 29, pp. 1–2.

Vygotsky, Lev Semenovich. 1978. *Mind in society: The development of higher psychological processes*. Edited by M. Cole. Cambridge, MA: Harvard University Press.

———. 2004. "Imagination and creativity in childhood." *Journal of Russian and East European Psychology* 42 (1): 7–97. Originally published in 1967.

Winnicott, Donald Woods. 1971. *Playing and reality*. New York: Basic Books.

Index

Anna R. Beresin is an Associate Professor at The University of the Arts in Philadelphia, the Director of Recess Access, and the author of *Recess Battles: Playing, Fighting, and Storytelling.*

5916 092